THE RIGHT WAY
TO KEEP DOGS

By the same author:

How to Have an Obedient Dog

In the same series:

How to Have a Well-Mannered Dog
The Right Way to Keep Cats
The Right Way to Keep Ponies
The Right Way to Keep Rabbits
The Right Way to Keep Hamsters
The Right Way to Keep Pet Fish

All uniform with this book

Where to find *Right Way*

Elliot *Right Way* take pride in our editorial quality, accuracy and value-for-money. Booksellers everywhere can rapidly obtain any *Right Way* book for you. If you have been particularly pleased with any one title, do please mention this to your bookseller as personal recommendation helps us enormously.

Please send to the address on the back of the title page opposite, a stamped, self-addressed envelope if you would like a copy of our *free catalogue*. Alternatively, you may wish to browse through our extensive range of informative titles arranged by subject on the Internet at **www.right-way.co.uk**

We welcome views and suggestions from readers as well as from prospective authors; do please write to us or e-mail: **info@right-way.co.uk**

THE RIGHT WAY
TO KEEP DOGS

INCLUDING HOW TO CHOOSE YOUR CANINE COMPANION

Jackie Marriott

RIGHT WAY

Typeset in 10/11pt Times by Letterpart Ltd., Reigate, Surrey.

Printed and bound in Great Britain by Cox & Wyman Ltd., Reading, Berkshire.

The *Right Way* series is published by Elliot Right Way Books, Brighton Road, Lower Kingswood, Tadworth, Surrey, KT20 6TD, U.K. For information about our company and the other books we publish, visit our website at www.right-way.co.uk.

ACKNOWLEDGEMENTS

My very grateful thanks to the following people for their contributions to this book:

Carol Baker, Nicola Barber, Bebe Bird, Andy Crumpton, Jean Foster, Pam Henderson, Angela Lee, Jan Lowrence, Diane Morgan, Alison Moss, Debbie Pe-ad, Sue Pope, Carol Ridge, Ann Rose, Stella Smith, Annette Standen, Maria Williams.

Special thanks to Sandy Enzerink BVMS MRCVS for once again checking the medical details, and for her continued support and care in looking after the health of my dogs.

DEDICATION

TO MIGGI

19.10.1989 – 20.5.2000

It was a special privilege to have a dog like her.

CONTENTS

PREFACE

The decision to get a dog for the first time can sometimes be made without enough proper thought. What does having a dog within the family actually involve? I consider the first few months of having a puppy in the house to be more disrupting than having a new baby: with a baby you at least have nine months to get used to the idea, plus you have loads of back-up and advice both from family members and the health services.

Anyone can get a dog. You don't have to take a test and you don't have to know anything about their habits or instincts. Often, the decision to have a dog in the family is based simply on seeing one or two good examples of well trained dogs, without having any idea of the hard work which has gone into getting those dogs to be so well behaved. Perhaps you have recollections from childhood of the family dog who was your 'best pal' who accompanied the family everywhere. As a child you will not have been involved in the basic groundwork which resulted in the dog being such a good friend to you. You may have been impressed by examples shown on television of perfectly trained dogs competing in the Obedience Championships at Crufts, or seemingly telepathic collies working sheep. What you will not have seen is the hard work and time involved in getting those dogs to such a high standard of obedience. You may have no aspirations to compete with or show your dog, but the responsibility and effort in rearing and training a pet dog properly, resulting in a well behaved family pet which is a pleasure to own, can be equally arduous.

The good news is that if *you* put the effort in, you too will end up having a new member of the family (albeit with four legs rather than two) who will be loyal, good company and non-judgmental. You will find that you make new friends, as dogs are great barrier-breakers. Exercising the dog will be good for you too; not only physically but mentally as well, giving you time out from the rigours of looking after the family or going to work.

This book is aimed at pointing out the possible pitfalls, making sure that you understand just what is involved in owning and being responsible for a dog, and helping that ownership to become a wonderful and lasting experience.

1

HOW TO CHOOSE THE RIGHT DOG FOR YOU

The first and most important decision you have to make is what sort of dog you want. Do you want a pedigree or crossbreed? Large or small? Dog or bitch? Long-coated or short-coated? Puppy or adult? Here are some things to consider.

Pedigree V Crossbreed

Pedigree Dogs
Pedigree dogs are classified in two categories – Sporting and Non-Sporting. Within these categories are different groups, i.e. Sporting – Hounds, Gundogs and Terriers; and Non-Sporting – Utility, Working, Pastoral and Toys. Within these groups are certain breeds of dogs which have been bred to perform a particular task or tasks. A more understandable definition for the new owner would be to describe dogs as having been bred deliberately to herd (Pastoral), to guard (Working), to flush out game, retrieve and hunt (Gundogs), to dig and kill vermin (Terriers), or to sniff (Hounds). Sometimes these individual tasks are combined, so that you get a dog who has evolved into one that will hunt, point and retrieve, such as Weimaraners or Pointers.

In addition to those traits already described, there are the dogs which humans in the past bred for use as almost a fashion accessory, such as the Dalmatian (Utility) – a very pretty dog which was used for trotting in between the rear wheels of carriages carrying the 'gentry', back in the seventeenth and eighteenth centuries. There are also dogs which were bred to kill or fight other animals, such as Bulldogs and Staffordshire Bull Terriers. (A full list of pedigree dogs begins on page 146.)

What you must appreciate is that dogs bred for any specific role will still retain some of their original instinct, even when kept as a family pet. As an example, Border Collies (Pastoral group) have been bred to herd sheep and work outdoors for anything up to twelve or fourteen hours a day. They are extremely active dogs, fixed on their task and can seemingly run forever. They are therefore not the ideal dog to live in a small flat, or to be left on their own for long periods of time, with just a half hour walk once a day! They *can* make good family dogs, provided they are properly trained and given plenty of interesting exercise, and preferably some form of "work" to do, like obedience competitions or agility exercises. If left to their own devices, they will "find" things to do to stimulate their brain – usually things that are completely undesirable in a family home! Left untrained, they will "herd" other people and dogs whilst on walks, and sometimes attempt to round up cyclists, runners or, worst of all, cars.

If you decide on a pedigree dog, you will be able to obtain advance information from breeders and from books. You can be virtually certain of the size he will become (if you are getting a puppy). You will be able to see what kind of coat he should have. Each individual breed has particular characteristics, which you can ascertain in advance. You will be able to enquire as to what, if any, genetic defects the breed is predisposed towards. You will know roughly the life expectancy of the breed. Within each individual breed you can of course get variations of temperament. As an example, the generally perceived idea is that Labradors and Golden Retrievers make perfect family pets, and German Shepherd Dogs (Alsatians) and Rottweilers are usually aggressive and should not be considered in a home with children. Whilst not wanting to upset owners or breeders of any of these breeds, I have come across some

Labradors and Retrievers who are extremely difficu
sometimes aggressive, and I have met several Rottweiler and
German Shepherds who are big softies. The point I am making
is that although the breed standard can be taken as a guide, the
temperament of the parents of the puppy, the way they are
reared, plus environmental factors, training and diet, all have an
effect on the eventual temperament of an individual dog.

Crossbreeds
The term 'crossbreed' can in itself be bewildering. A first-
cross dog is the result of a mating between two specific breeds,
for example a Labrador and a Collie, becoming a Labrador/
Collie cross. A second-cross dog is less easy to define. Some
will say it is the result of a mating between a specific breed and
a first-cross bred dog, like a Labrador and a Labrador/Collie
cross. Others will say that a second-cross dog is the result of a
mating between *two* first-cross bred dogs, Labrador/Collie to
Labrador/Collie. And so it continues – are you confused yet?
The simplest definition is to accept that after several out-
crosses, you end up with a Mongrel, i.e. a mixture of several
breeds. That being the case, if you decide on a puppy, you will
not necessarily know what size it will grow to, what type of
coat it will have, and what character traits it will possess.
However, devoted crossbred/mongrel owners will tell you how
much hardier their dog is compared to a pedigree, which is
generally true, because any of the physical weaknesses of the
pedigree dogs originally involved in the crossbreeding tend to
become 'diluted' as each out-cross is made. They will say that
they are much more loving, less highly strung and tend to fit
more easily into a family environment. Having myself owned
crossbred dogs, mongrel dogs and pedigree dogs, I would say
that it comes down to personal choice and that each type of dog
is special in his own way.

What Size Dog?
Probably the first factor to be taken into account is your living
accommodation and lifestyle. A large, active dog, such as a
Retriever or German Shepherd, is not generally suited to live

in a flat. Ideally, every dog should have access to a garden, but some smaller breeds can adapt well to life in the confines of a flat, provided of course that they are taken out several times a day. A few of the giant breeds, such as the Great Dane or Bernese Mountain Dog, can cope very well within a smaller house, as their activity ratio is much less than, say, a Spaniel or Collie.

Another factor to take into account is how long will the dog live. Generally speaking, the smaller breeds live much longer than the larger ones. Could you cope with only having your dog for seven or eight years, which is the lifespan of some large dogs? Alternatively, some smaller breeds live well into their teens – they may still be around when the children have left home.

If your family leads a very social lifestyle, it is far easier to take a smaller dog out for the day, in the car or on the bus or train. Visitors to the house may not be quite so daunted being met with something like a Cavalier King Charles Spaniel, compared to the visual and physical impact that an Irish Wolfhound makes. Even if your own children could cope with a large breed, could your children's friends, who will undoubtedly be visiting the house, cope with being met by a dog as tall as themselves?

Exercise
One very commonly held misconception is that smaller dogs require less exercise than bigger dogs. In fact, most of the smaller breeds can take as much, if not more, exercise than their bigger cousins. The larger breeds such as German Shepherds and Retrievers do need plenty of exercise – at least two good hour long walks off the lead a day – but the Poodle, Spaniel or Terrier can be just as demanding. Giant breeds can require less, as they tend to be more Saloon car than Sports! Even then, they can still walk for several miles a day (when they are fully grown). Exercise is not just about tiring the dog out, either! It should be a stimulating and rewarding time for the dog, plus an excellent opportunity to help you to interact with the dog, aiding the bonding process.

Dog or Bitch?

From a purely practical viewpoint, males are easier to own as they don't come into season twice a year! Obviously, you can have a bitch spayed, which can cost anything from £50 to £150 depending on the size of the bitch and also what part of the country you live in, as veterinary costs vary considerably. Letting a female breed can be costly too, and should only be undertaken by the expert (see page 94). Most male dogs are easier to live with if you have them neutered (see page 95), and, contrary to one popularly held belief, it only improves their character, rather than changing it for the worse. Male dogs tend to urinate more often than bitches, and this can be mildly irritating when walking down the road, for example, with the dog cocking his leg on every lamp post or tree! Bitches will be smaller than dogs, which may be a factor in making up your mind as to which sex to choose. Very broadly speaking, it is my experience that bitches are more compliant than dogs, so for the first time owner it may be best to choose a female. Although individual bitches can turn out to be aggressive, they are generally more passive than the males. On a personal level, I have found that the males tend to be slightly more "devoted" to individual family members, which is very good for the ego of that particular person, but may not be ideal if you want a dog that will bond well with the whole family.

Puppy V Adult

Puppies

If you leave the children to decide, they will undoubtedly want a puppy! To a child, a puppy is cuddly, cute and fun. As it is the adults in the family who will have to do the feeding, training and clearing up after the puppy, then *they* must really want a puppy too. The advantage of getting a puppy is that, provided you have picked the right type of dog for you and have found out all you can about that particular breed or crossbreed, then you will at least have some knowledge of what to expect. You will also be starting a clean slate with, hopefully, no learned behavioural problems or phobias to deal with. A puppy will also be easier to fit in within the family, as he will be growing up and learning with your children, and will not have any previous, possibly unpleasant, experience of children. It will also be easier for the puppy to integrate with any other pets you may have, such as cats or rabbits, for the same reason. The disadvantages of getting a puppy are that he will not be housetrained, you may have a few sleepless nights to contend with as the puppy settles in, they can be costly to rear, and you will have to teach him everything – puppies come as a blank canvas, and it is up to you to paint the picture!

Adult Dogs

Some people would opt for an adult dog, possibly from a rescue centre, for economic or sentimental reasons. There is a good case to be made for getting a rescue dog, in as much as that he needs a home, but you have to take great care that you know the real reasons why the dog needs to be re-homed. You cannot be certain of the dog's temperament in any given situation, most importantly how the dog will adapt to living with your children, if you have any. You may still encounter some of the same problems as you would with a puppy, but the positive side of having an adult dog is that he will probably already be house-trained, may already have some basic training instilled, and will not involve the same rearing costs as with a puppy (see page 19).

Coat Type

All dogs, whether they have a short or long coat, will need regular grooming. Short-coated breeds will need a good brushing about twice a week, whereas the long-coated variety really need daily attention to prevent the coat from becoming matted or tangled. If your family routine does not allow for the time this will involve, then pick a short-coated dog. After a wet walk, the short coat takes much less time to dry – the long coat may need attention not only from a towel, but also from a hair drier. Some breeds will also require clipping by a professional groomer, and this of course adds considerably to the overall expense of keeping a dog. Irrespective of coat type, most breeds shed their hair continually, so regular attention with the brush and comb is essential.

Individual Home Environment

When it comes to choosing the type of dog suitable for your family, you need to take into account not only the size of your living accommodation, but also your family routine. If everyone is out of the house all day, it is not an ideal situation for any dog. Some people do manage, by having a family member or friend regularly drop in to visit and/or walk the dog. You could employ a professional dog walker, but this will add to the expense of keeping the dog (see *Overall Costs in Owning a Dog*, page 19). Remember that dogs are highly social animals, so spending most of their daily life alone is far from satisfactory, and will also make training and bonding much more difficult. All dogs have to learn to spend some time on their own, but this should be the lesser rather than the greater part of their lives.

Children

Children and dogs can form wonderful bonds which enhance the life of both the child and the dog. Having a dog can teach the child about responsibility too, if he or she is given simple tasks involving caring for the dog – provided the child is properly supervised, of course. Children should NOT be given the responsibility of walking or training the dog. Even when held on a lead, dogs can be unpredictable on occasion, and, in the worst case scenario, the child could end up being harmed. If the children are still at the toddler stage, great care must be taken to ensure that the child and dog are never left alone unsupervised. Young children can be unpredictable too, and can unintentionally provoke a dog into becoming aggressive. Generally, it is wise to wait until the children are older, at least until they start school, before embarking on dog ownership.

The Impact of a Dog in Your Home

If you are very houseproud, DON'T GET A DOG! Dogs will shed their coat continually and usually have two 'bumper moults' a year as well! Even daily use of the vacuum cleaner will still not remove every trace. Dog hair retains grease, and you will notice that all surfaces at dog height – corners of walls, doors, cupboards etc. – will need cleaning regularly to remove the grease that is wiped on when the dog rubs past. Dogs get muddy – sometimes from just being in the garden – and guess where that mud ends up? Usually when you have just finishing washing the floor or vacuuming! Dog hair sticks to clothes and furniture too. Dogs have "accidents" indoors sometimes (particularly puppies). Can you cope with clearing up diarrhoea or vomit? Of course, you also have to be prepared to clean up after your dog has been to the toilet whilst on exercise.

Some dogs salivate profusely – Newfoundlands, Bloodhounds and St. Bernards are just some of the breeds which are particularly slobbery dogs – and that saliva can end up in the most unusual places! Dogs get fleas if not treated regularly with preparations from the vet. It doesn't take long for those fleas to take over your house. As well as these fleas living with you, they will bite you as well! Have I put anybody off yet? There's more to come! Puppies, and some older dogs, will chew anything and everything left on the floor. Clothes, toys, shoes, slippers may all be demolished if left lying about. Food left on work tops will be fair game to the agile dog. Crisps and sandwiches left on the coffee table will disappear! Furniture and carpets will be chewed if puppies are left unsupervised – some older dogs will chew too.

If after reading the above you're still determined to get a dog – GREAT. At least you won't be able to say that you weren't warned!

Holidays

When the family is planning their holiday, you obviously have to decide if the dog is going too. There are many places in Great Britain where dogs are positively welcomed but, if it is not possible to take the dog with you – perhaps you are going abroad to a country where the Pet Passport System is not accepted (see page 113) – then you will have to make arrangements for the dog to be cared for whilst you are away. This could involve putting him in a boarding kennel, or arranging a house/dog sitter. Unless you can get a family member or friend to do this for you, either option will add considerably to the costs of your holiday. Either way, you will need to book the kennel or sitter well in advance. If you decide that boarding kennels are the right option for you, do go and visit several before booking, so that you can look around and ask questions. Even if the kennels are personally recommended, you should still visit them beforehand – perhaps they have had staff or management changes which may have changed the overall care on offer.

If you are going to be boarding your dog, it is a good idea to book the dog in for a short stay first, perhaps over a weekend, so that if there are going to be any problems, you will be at home to deal with them. Any little habits or phobias can be identified, so that when it comes to leaving the dog for a couple of weeks, the kennel staff will be aware of what to expect. This also acclimatises the dog to being confined and away from you for a short time, after which you come and collect him. When it is time for the longer period of being left in the kennels, the dog will have a remembered association with being left previously, and also that, after being left, you returned.

From a security aspect, if your dog either goes into kennels, or accompanies you on holiday, it is a good idea to put a temporary identity disc on the dog's collar with either the kennel address or your holiday home address. If the dog should stray from either, and only has your home address on, the finder of the dog will be unable to get in touch.

Overall Costs in Owning a Dog
Some of the cost of ownership will vary depending on the size and breed of dog you choose, simply because small dogs will eat less than big dogs, and pedigree dogs are not considered

quite so hardy as crossbreeds, so may need more veterinary attention. Puppies will cost more initially too, with the cost of purchase and so on. Also, as previously mentioned, veterinary fees can vary enormously from one part of the country to the other. It is impossible to give an exact figure of what your dog will cost you during its life, but to give you some idea, let's assume that your dog will live an average of 12 years, and that you are buying a medium sized pedigree puppy, such as a Springer Spaniel.

Purchase Price	Between £100 and £1000 for a Pedigree
Initial Vaccination Course	£40.00
Annual Booster Vaccination: £26.00 per year × 12	£312.00
Worm Treatment: £16.00 per year × 12	£192.00
Flea Treatment: £40 per year × 12	£480.00
Veterinary Insurance: average £60.00 per year × 12	£720.00
Spaying Bitch	£107.00
Castrating Dog	£75.00
Food: average £1.00 per day × 365 days × 12	£4,380.00
Identity Discs	£5.00
Micro-chipping	£26.00
Dog Training Classes	£50.00

Professional Groomer: approx £25.00 every 8/10 weeks,

£125.00 per year × 12	£1500.00

Grooming Equipment:
brush and comb   £10.00

Collars and Leads   £20.00

Bed and Bedding   £50.00

Toys: the sky's the limit, but initial
puppy toys approx   £25.00

Indoor Kennel   £100.00

Boarding Kennels: approx £8.00 per day

14 days = £112.00 × 12	£1344.00

Extra Costs: Medical treatment (even with insurance you have to pay an excess – usually around £30 per condition). Damage caused through chewing and house training accidents. This could be a minor expense, or could be replacement of a three seater leather settee! These costs may vary considerably with individual establishments and in different areas of the country.

By doing a few sums, you can see that just in the first year of owning your dog, and excluding the purchase price, the known expenses can be around £764, and that is not allowing for boarding kennels, or the purchase of an indoor kennel, or a groomer or going to training classes. Without taking into account any price rises (and again excluding the purchase price, boarding kennels, an indoor kennel, grooming and training costs), assuming your dog lives for 12 years he will cost you between £6,000 and £6,500. And don't forget those unknown costs – damage to furniture etc, and medical bills not covered by insurance.

2

WHERE TO BUY?

Having made all the choices and decisions about what type of dog to get, you now have yet another decision to make – where do you get him from?

Registered Breeders
You can obtain a list of registered breeders of the particular breed you want from The Kennel Club (see Appendix, page 155). They will send you a list of breeders in your area, but please be aware that this list will not necessarily mean that those breeders have puppies available at that moment. You may also see breeders advertising in the canine press or even sometimes in your local paper. Possibly the best way to get details of breeders, and also advice about the breed you have chosen, is to contact the Kennel Club and ask for the name and address of the Secretary of the Breed club for that breed. It is my experience that secretaries of such clubs are more than willing to offer advice, usually over the telephone, about their special breed, and will advise where a litter of puppies may be available. They are also usually very honest in pointing out the possible problems associated with their breed, as it is in the Breed club's interest to ensure that their breed is properly represented and they know that all breeds have some faults, albeit maybe minor.

Some breeders are also prepared to sell adult dogs as well as puppies. They may have bred a litter and kept back one or two of the puppies from sale to see if they develop as suitable dogs for showing. In the trade this is called "running on". If the puppy does not then develop with sufficient potential for the show ring, the breeder will sell him on. Although there is nothing wrong with this practice in principle, you *may* end up with a dog of between 6 and 12 months old who has only known life in a kennel environment, who has not been socialised or had any training, and who is still living with his natural mother. The behavioural problems that this can bring may make you want to think again before going down that particular path.

You may also be offered a puppy on "breeding terms". Some financial reduction will be made for this, in exchange for your agreeing to allow the dog or bitch to be used for breeding. This could involve, with a bitch puppy, allowing the breeder to choose a stud dog and mate him to your bitch when old enough. The breeder may insist that the bitch returns to him for whelping (giving birth), and the breeder may also take one or all of the puppies for selling on, and may ask for all or some of the selling price of the puppies. If you take a male dog on breeding terms, depending on the arrangement, you may find that you are expected to entertain many bitches (and their owners), for several hours at a time whilst dog and bitch are mated, without any financial compensation or gain. Be it dog or bitch, these types of arrangements can be beset with problems, particularly for the inexperienced dog owner, and my advice would be to steer clear.

Do try and see more than one litter of puppies from more than one breeder before making your choice. Every breeder has his own thoughts on the right way to breed and raise a litter, so by making comparisons you should come up with the right choice of breeder *for you*.

Pet Shops/Pet Superstores
Many of these establishments are very well run, but generally speaking the puppies are litters which have been bought in. You will not be able to see the mother of the puppies, and neither will you have any knowledge of how they have been raised. There is also the risk of "impulse buying", or worse still, buying a puppy because you feel sorry for it. My strong advice would be don't even go and look – you will have to be very hard hearted not to want to bring a puppy home with you!

Buying from a Friend or Member of the Family

This can often be a very satisfactory way of buying a puppy, because you will probably know the mother of the puppies and the environment into which the puppies have been born. Of course, you will still need to ensure that the parents of the puppies have been checked for genetic defects etc, and that the temperament of both parents is as it should be.

Difficulties can occur with this type of purchase if you discover a medical problem with the puppy shortly after he arrives home with you. You may feel unable to mention the matter, as you don't want to fall out with your friend or relative. On the other hand, it may be that you are *more* upset because they *are* friends/family and, having taken issue with them, you end up falling out. Either way may present you with a dilemma. If you choose this route for obtaining your puppy, make sure that you have all the necessary paperwork and information about the puppy, as you would expect from a registered breeder. In other words, keep it as business-like as possible.

Local Advertising

Most local newspapers have a pet column where you will see puppies and sometimes adult dogs offered for sale. The 'Free Sheet' type of newspaper particularly seems to specialise in this type of advertising. Although there is nothing intrinsically wrong in this, some of the people advertising puppies may have little or no experience in breeding, and may simply have bred from their own pet bitch because they think it is "good for her to have a litter" (see *Breeding*, page 96). They may not have had the bitch checked for any inherited genetic defects, nor may they have enquired too closely as to the temperament of the stud dog, or whether he had also had the required checks done.

If you see an older puppy or dog being advertised for sale, do make sure you know the real reasons behind the sale. It may be for a genuine reason, such as the owner moving abroad, or a marriage break-up, but not everyone is completely truthful, and it could be that you end up buying a problem dog.

It's not all doom and despondency though, and I have known some lovely puppies bought from newspaper adverts.

Just be extremely careful and ask lots of questions. Once again, you should still get all the relevant paperwork and information, as you would expect from a registered breeder.

Puppy Farms
Sadly, puppy farming still exists and, although rarely sold directly from where they are bred, litters from puppy farms are often bought by retail outlets or advertised in the newspapers. Basically, puppy farms are places where several bitches are kept and used mainly as breeding machines, often having a litter twice a year, for several years running. Frequently, the bitches are first bred from when still immature, are bred from irrespective of temperament or genetic faults, and are not given the close attention that a bitch needs when rearing a litter. Because the bitch is bred from far too often, she will not be in the prime condition needed to rear a litter and consequently the puppies may not obtain all the nourishment from her necessary for healthy growth. The puppies are usually kept away from human contact and home environments, and are therefore not properly socialised or acclimatised to living with or being in the company of people. The result is that they are often very nervous or aggressive. There are always, of course, exceptions to every rule, but in the main puppies bred in such a way should be avoided.

Rescue Centres
Pedigree and Crossbred adult dogs and puppies end up in rescue kennels for many reasons: frequently because not enough thought had been given by the previous owner before getting the dog; a pitfall that hopefully you will avoid by reading this book! Rescue centres are run very professionally these days, with great care given to the health and mental well-being of the dogs in their care. Obviously, spending days or weeks on end in a kennel is not good for any dog, and however hard the staff try, in a kennel environment it is not possible to reproduce the kind of attention that a dog will receive within a loving family home.

As much care as possible is taken in getting a full history from the previous owner when a dog is handed in – of course sometimes people are not completely truthful, so the full reasons may never be known. With stray dogs, no previous history is available to the rescue centre, but in all instances, the staff will do as much assessment as is possible while the dog is in their care, to ensure that he is re-homed appropriately.

When a litter of puppies is either born at the centre, or brought in for whatever reason, it may not be obvious what breed of dog the puppies are. An educated guess is made by the staff, going on size, colouring and sometimes temperament of the puppies. All too frequently the litter is cross-bred, and often will end up being described as, for example, a Collie Cross. Given that within the Collie breed there are several different varieties, ranging from the small Shetland Sheepdog to the much bigger Rough Collie, and from the Border Collie to the Bearded Collie, it really is pot luck what you may end up with in the way of size and temperament.

If you decide that you would like to give a home to either a puppy or adult dog from a rescue organisation, be prepared for them to ask you lots of questions! As well as doing their best to match the right dog with the right family, they will also want to avoid the situation where a newly re-homed dog is returned after a few weeks because the family cannot cope. One of the biggest rescue kennels in the country takes in over 10,000 dogs per year. You can also expect to have a home check prior to being accepted, and also for them to refuse you if there are very young children at home. Most rescue centres also follow up on dogs which have been re-homed with an after-care visit. I know that some people can feel rather aggrieved at the questions and limitations imposed, but the centres would not be doing their job properly if they accepted everyone on face value. They have the task of re-homing a possibly already traumatised dog, and need to know that not only will it be properly and lovingly looked after, but that the potential new owners are prepared for the possible problems which may occur.

At my training club at least a third of the dogs which attend are from rescue centres, and I have seen many times how, with the proper care, a 'rescue' dog can be successfully integrated into a new home.

3

SELECTING YOUR PUPPY FROM THE LITTER

If you have decided on a puppy rather than an adult dog, have agreed which sex you are having and have chosen the breeder, the exciting moment will then arrive when you go to see the puppies for the first time. Don't be disappointed if the breeder wants you to wait until the puppies are about four weeks old – this is the best time to see them. Any earlier and it is difficult to tell them apart, and it is also stressful for both Mum and pups to have prospective buyers around, not to mention the risk of bringing infection into the litter. At four weeks, the pups will have eyes open, be well on the way to being weaned, and will look more like miniature versions of the adult dog. They will also be more active and less likely to sleep all the way through your visit! For the first visit the breeder may well ask that just the adults in the family come, again so that the bitch and her pups are not too stressed.

Bearing in mind that you cannot determine the sex of a bitch's unborn puppies, you may well not have a choice of puppy. If that is the case, then it is up to you whether you decide to take what is on offer, or wait for that particular breeder, or another of your choice, to breed another litter – always bearing in mind that the same thing could happen again.

Choosing Your Puppy

The size of the litter and ratio of dogs to bitches can play a part in the overall temperament of the litter. The absolute ideal would be six puppies, comprising three dogs and three bitches. Size-wise, six would be easy for the mother to rear, and six puppies would have just enough competition for food and toys to allow them to develop as social animals. An even balance between the sexes often gives a more clearly defined difference in temperament between males and females. If a litter is predominantly male, for example, you may find that any bitches will have more of a masculine temperament. Likewise, a predominantly female litter with only one or two males may result in the males being of a softer temperament. This is not necessarily a bad thing, but simply something to be aware of.

Small litters, say two or three, or large litters of twelve, are not a bad sign, but could make your choice either more difficult, if there are several to choose from, or more restricted, if the litter is small. Occasionally, there may only be one puppy, often sadly caused by puppies being stillborn, or by illness wiping out most of the litter. A single puppy will undoubtedly get the very best nutrition from the bitch, as there will be no competition, so he or she will probably be big and healthy. From a temperament point of view, not having any siblings will mean that he may not learn to play, or learn how to interact with other dogs, so he might be either a bit on the shy side, or could end up not liking other dogs. Having had experience of owning an only puppy, my dog developed into a devoted family dog, but one who wasn't particularly concerned with interacting with other dogs or people, but who was not aggressive. I had to teach him how to play, which was quite difficult, but he learned eventually. I also know of other single puppies who have developed into the "life and soul of the party", which only goes to show that a single puppy is not necessarily to be avoided, but may just need more careful thought as to how he is handled.

Before you even look at the puppies, try and have a good look at, and interact with, the mother of the puppies. You should already have ascertained how old the mother is. Ideally she should be at least two years of age, which gives her the chance to mature properly before being burdened with motherhood. If the bitch is under a year, she may well be too immature, both physically and mentally, to rear a litter well. It is quite usual for the bitch to be slightly apprehensive of you while her puppies are around, as she will obviously be protective of them, so try and arrange to see her first without the puppies. Although there are many factors which form a puppy's temperament, the pups will inherit many traits from *both* parents, and learn much from their mother whilst in the litter. It will often not be possible to see the father of the puppies, as frequently the owner of the bitch does not own the stud dog. Your assessment has therefore to be based on the temperament of the mother. If she is fearful of humans, the pups may well be too. If she is frightened of loud noises, the pups will pick that up from her. If she is calm and gentle, willing to socialise with you, she will pass that attitude on to her pups.

Ask the breeder whether the pups are being acclimatised to household noises, such as washing machines and vacuum cleaners. Have they been handled regularly? If the pups are kept outside the house, find out if they have ever been brought indoors. If the puppies are being kept isolated from normal household sights and sounds, you will have a harder job of settling the puppy you choose into your home environment.

Check the overall condition of both the litter and the mother. Are the eyes and noses clean? Is there any sneezing or coughing? Look at the puppies' coats. Are they clean and pleasant smelling? Is the area where they are being kept clean and free from stale urine and faeces?

Assuming you have a choice, picking *the one* for you is certainly not an exact science, but there are some general guidelines that are worth considering. Above everything, temperament *must* be the most important factor. Try not to be influenced by a "pretty face". Quite apart from anything else, frequently the best looking puppy does not grow into the best looking dog. Even if the puppy does turn out to be very good looking, if the temperament doesn't match the looks, you could end up with problems.

Take into account your living arrangements and family routine. If your family is, for example, quite noisy, then you do not want to pick the quietest puppy in the litter – that puppy will do best in a calmer environment. Neither do you want the noisiest puppy in the litter if your home life is of a quiet nature. For first time dog owners, I would certainly not recommend the biggest, pushiest puppy. That pup has developed his character by demanding his own way amongst his litter mates, and, possibly through sending out aggressive signals to his siblings, has gained first and best position at the 'milk bar', first choice of food on offer, and possession of the best toys. You can therefore expect him to try the same tactics with his new human family. Unless you are fairly experienced with dogs, you may be in for quite a rough ride with this type of puppy.

There are some simple tests that you can do to get an idea of the pup's temperament, but it would be courteous to explain first to the breeder what you intend doing. While sitting on the floor and cuddling the pup, *gently* turn the pup onto his back and place him on the floor, keeping him in place with very soft pressure. You can expect the pup to struggle for a few seconds, but he should then relax and be happy to lie there, while you gently stroke him, for at least 10 seconds. This shows compliance, and indicates that the puppy will accept that you are in charge, making training that much easier. If the puppy continues to struggle throughout this procedure, it could be that this puppy will not adapt so well to being taught to lie down, or to stay.

Having played with the puppies, stand up, turn your back and walk away a few feet. See which puppy follows you immediately. Puppies that follow tend to be more sociable with humans, to enjoy human contact, and are unlikely to be shy of strangers. Similarly, throw the toys for the puppies and observe which is the quickest to chase. You want the pup to be interested in the toy, but the puppy who hangs on to it and won't allow the others to share is likely to grow up to be more possessive. This could show up later as aggressiveness with food, stealing and running off with things, or taking control of a chair and refusing to move.

Gently clap your hands and encourage the puppies to come to you. The puppy that hangs back and is reluctant to come to you may be very timid and unsure of coming to a stranger, *or* may be very independent and not feel the need to interact with humans. Either one does not bode well for a family dog. The puppy who gets to you first will probably be very sociable, so be prepared for that one to want to speak to everyone when out walking in the park. That isn't necessarily a fault, it is simply a case of whether that is acceptable to you. The puppy who appears to think for a few seconds and assess the situation before approaching is possibly a better choice. This puppy will be friendly, but not 'over the top' with visitors.

When you have finally made your decision, if the puppies have identical markings, you can expect the breeder to mark your chosen puppy in some way – sometimes they put a tiny spot of nail varnish on the tip of your chosen puppy's ear, sometimes they will cut a little fur off from somewhere on the puppy's body, and sometimes they will put a little coloured ribbon collar around your puppy's neck. It is a good idea for you to take several photographs of your puppy from various angles – puppies change rapidly, and the more means of identification you have the better.

Collecting the Puppy
Probably the next thing you will want to know from the breeder is *when* you can have your puppy. The first few weeks of a puppy's life are crucial to his eventual development. He is changing and learning daily. If the pup leaves his natural mother too early, some vital socialising techniques will not have been learned. Up until seven weeks of age, the pup needs both Mum and siblings to continue the development of his inter-canine skills and he is still vulnerable. The ideal time for the pup to develop new bonds, and for transferring loyalty, is between seven and eight weeks. At this age the puppy is neurologically complete and able to learn, whilst still being physically unable to compete with adult dogs.

There are still some breeders who will not let their puppies leave until ten weeks or over. Puppies who stay with their natural mum and siblings beyond eight weeks frequently suffer from the lack of those vital two weeks of socialising with other humans and in other situations. As a result, they may end up shy or fearful, and have far more difficulty in adapting to their change of environment.

4

PREPARING FOR THE ARRIVAL OF YOUR DOG

Deciding on a Name
During the three to four weeks from selecting your puppy to bringing him home, you will need to make several decisions. The first is a choice of name. This is obviously a very personal thing, but there are still some things to bear in mind before you finally select your puppy's name.

Dogs can learn a variety of sounds which will become associated with various things, but the most important is his name sound. You will be using the puppy's name before every command you give him, and you therefore need to choose a sound that is easily picked up by the pup. Try to keep the name short, as a longer name is more difficult for the pup to isolate. As an example, "Bilbo Baggins" may sound very amusing, but is extremely hard for the pup to pick up on. Try to choose a name with a clearly defined beginning and end, like "Topsy", which gives a nice clear "Toh" sound at the start and a "See" sound at the end. Another example of a difficult sound for the dog to hear would be "Anna" – a soft beginning and a soft ending. "Fritz", on the other hand, has a hard 'Frr' and the beginning and a 'Tss' and the end, being an easier sound for the dog to isolate.

Most people try to be original in their choice of name for their dog, as they like to be different. Please don't try and be too different though – the pup may have so much difficulty learning it that in the end he just ignores it altogether!

Naming an Adult Dog
If you are getting an adult dog, he will already have a name. You may want to keep that name, but the dog can learn a new name sound if you decide that you don't like the original one. It is particularly worth considering changing the name if the dog has been previously ill treated, as the name is a permanent connection in the mind of the dog with the perpetrator of that treatment. Try to use the same criteria as described for naming a puppy. Once you have decided on the new name, join it onto the end of the old name each time you speak to the dog. For example, if the dog is called Buster, and you want to change it to Ben, you would say "BusterBen". At first, place more emphasis on the "Buster" part, and then slowly, over a couple of weeks, begin to emphasise the "Ben" sound. After another couple of weeks, perhaps even sooner, you can drop the Buster altogether. Make sure that each time the dog is fed, or given a treat, the name is used – the dog will learn much quicker if food is involved!

What Will the Dog or Puppy Sleep in?
Before you go and spend a considerable amount on a dog bed, give some thought to what puppies tend to do when they start teething – they CHEW. Adult dogs may well be feeling unsettled when they are re-homed, and this could prompt them into chewing too. If you have spent money on a lovely bed and bedding, you will be none too impressed if it is all destroyed within weeks! It is probably best to start off with a substantial cardboard box, having checked that it does not have any sharp staples or sticky tape still attached. Put a couple of blankets, or possibly a piece of veterinary bedding, in the box. Provided it is placed in a warm, draught proof position, this will suffice as a perfectly acceptable bed until the puppy has passed through the chewing stage. Then you can go and get the 'state of the art' dog bed if you wish!

Where Will the Bed be Placed?

Where the dog or puppy sleeps is often the source of many an argument, so try and get it sorted before you bring the dog home. Even dog experts can disagree about where the dog should sleep! Some people will say that the kitchen is the obvious place – it is usually one of the warmest rooms in the house, often the floor surface is more easily cleaned should there be any 'accidents', there is no expensive furniture for the dog to chew (always assuming he doesn't start on the kitchen units!). During the daytime the kitchen tends to be the hub of family life and as such the puppy will be easy to supervise, even when in his bed.

Other experts will tell you that as the dog is a pack animal, the obvious place for him to sleep is with the head of the pack, i.e. you. If you allow the dog free run of the bedroom at night time, I can virtually guarantee that you will have some sleepless nights in front of you!

My particular preference is for a slight compromise – I like to have my dogs in with me at night time, because I do subscribe to the pack theory, but I do not feel happy about a puppy being able to roam about, possibly getting into danger by chewing electric wires and so on, while I am asleep (assuming I am able to sleep, that is!). I therefore put any puppy I have in an indoor kennel at bed time.

Indoor Kennels – New Puppies

Get any thought of a huge wooden construction with an arched roof out of your head! An indoor kennel is constructed from rigid welded galvanised mesh, with four sides (one as a door), a floor and a roof. It provides a completely enclosed, see-through and safe den for your dog. I know that some people are initially horrified at the thought of confining their puppy within a steel "cage". I can promise you that your puppy will very quickly accept such confinement. Indeed, dogs are natural denning animals: if left to their own devices they will usually create their own dens around your home without your realising it. Under a table or chair, in a corner of the room – all these areas become a den for the dog.

An indoor kennel provides a completely enclosed, see-through and safe den for your dog.

The indoor kennel should be big enough for the dog to stand up, turn around and stretch. One end should house the dog's bed, and the other should contain a bowl of water (fixed to the side of the pen if possible). You can either make the kennel yourself, or purchase one from a specialist company, either through your pet shop or from suppliers who advertise in the dog press. The kennel should be made so that it completely folds flat, enabling you to move it around as you wish. For example, during the day the kennel can be in the kitchen, then moved to the bedroom at night.

Indoor kennels have a couple of very definite advantages. It is rare for a puppy to soil his own sleeping area, so the indoor kennel is a very positive aid in house-training your puppy. Of course, the puppy must first be allowed access to his toilet area before being put in the kennel and you can expect some very early morning starts for the first few weeks! The other huge advantage of acclimatising a puppy to regular periods of confinement is that when the puppy has to be left alone for an hour or so during the day, you can put him into his kennel and he will not have access to the areas he is likely to want to chew. Make sure that during these periods he has one or two safe, sensible toys to occupy himself with (see *Toys*, page 38). It will also be very useful when your children and their friends are rampaging around the house – and No! – not as somewhere to shut them in! The puppy can be put in his kennel to stop him getting over-excited, and also to protect him from the possible unwanted attention of the children.

Many dog owners continue with the indoor kennel throughout the dog's life. If that is your intention, buy or build a kennel that is going to be big enough for your dog when he is fully grown. With my own breed – Bernese Mountain Dogs – the kennel I use whilst they are puppies is 4ft long, 3ft wide and 3ft high. Bearing in mind that they are only in the kennel when they are resting, this is quite big enough for them during the first six to nine months, and then I add on panels (3ft × 3ft), as necessary, to form an extension run. (Details of stockists for indoor and extension panels are given on page 155.)

The indoor kennel should not be used to house the dog for the greater part of his day. It should simply be used as a secure area in which to leave him at bed time, when you are out for an hour or so, or when you are busy indoors and cannot supervise him, until he is 'housetrained' in every sense of the word. With the extensions previously described, it is acceptable to leave the adult dog in the kennel for two to three hours at a time, but certainly not all day long.

Lastly, please do not use the indoor kennel as a place where you "send" the dog to as punishment. The indoor kennel should be a place of comfort, calm and security – a place to which the dog has access twenty-four hours a day, so that, if he chooses, he can escape to his den for some rest and relaxation.

Indoor Kennels – Adult Dogs
If you are re-homing an adult dog, who may never have been in an indoor kennel, you will need to acclimatise the dog slowly to being confined – don't just shut him in there and expect him not to complain!

Have the kennel positioned in the place where it is to stay, set up with bedding and so on, the same as described for a puppy. Leave the kennel door open all the time. For the first few days, feed every meal to the dog inside the kennel, but *do not shut the door*. Place some interesting toys inside and slowly you will find that the dog goes into the kennel on his own accord, perhaps even lying down for a while. Don't be tempted to rush over and slam the door shut. Only when the dog has shown he is perfectly relaxed being inside, for up to twenty minutes, should you very casually push the door closed, but do not secure it. Keep the door closed for ten minutes, then just as casually, open it again. If, when you start to close the door, the dog immediately tries to rush out, don't react – let him come out if he wants to. Just wait until he is relaxed enough to venture in on his own once more, and start again.

So long as you don't rush the dog, within two to three weeks he will be quite happy to have the door secured behind him, and will remain in the kennel for an hour or so. Gradually build up the time until you can leave him in there whilst you go out for a couple of hours. As long as he has had a chance to relieve himself before going into the kennel, and has something safe to amuse himself with whilst in there, it will quickly become part of his routine.

Toys
All puppies and most adult dogs need toys to amuse themselves when left alone, and to interact with you during a 'playtime'. There is a multitude of choice in the pet shops, but you don't necessarily need to spend a fortune on things for your dog to play with. The cardboard roll innards of kitchen towel roll or toilet roll are super toys, and are something you usually throw away anyway. The dog can play with and chew it and you can use the cardboard roll to play "fetch games" with the dog. Empty cardboard boxes are also great fun – after you have removed any staples or sticky paper, of course.

A couple of toys which you may like to buy are the 'educational' type. An example of these is a plastic cube which is hollow inside and has small holes on the outside. You can 'post' small treats inside the cube, and, as the puppy plays with it, every so often a treat appears. This can keep them amused for ages. There is also a rubber cone-shaped toy, advertised as being indestructible, with hollow insides. If you fill the hollow with soft dog food, it will keep the puppy concentrated for quite a while, as he licks the food out, much like a marrow bone, but safer as there is no risk of bone splinters being ingested.

Please don't be tempted to give an adult dog or a puppy old shoes or slippers to play with. Apart from the danger of the dog swallowing them – possibly causing a severe internal blockage – it also teaches them to eat shoes, as they won't distinguish between old and new ones!

Collars and Leads – Puppies

You will initially need to buy just a soft collar and lead for your puppy. Don't be tempted to buy the best in the shop – it will only last for a few weeks, as the pup will soon outgrow it. It is basically needed to acclimatise the puppy to wearing a collar and being held gently on a lead. The collar should be put on the puppy as soon as you have brought him home. The lead should be not be put on for a couple of weeks, and then used as described in the section *Walking on the Lead*, page 75.

Collars and Leads – Adult Dogs

A nice leather or flat nylon collar, plus good quality leather lead, are ideal for the adult dog. As soon as you take over ownership, you will need to fit a visible means of identification on to the dog's collar (see *Identification*, page 111). If the dog you take on has already learned to pull hard when on a lead, an alternative to an ordinary collar is the head collar which is now readily available. The head collar is very similar to the halter worn by horses (not the bridle and bit type!) and although it can take the dog a little while to become accustomed to something around his head, it has proved very successful with some dogs who were previously strenuous pullers (see *Training*, page 71).

Feeding Your Dog or Puppy

You will need to have a supply of the food which the breeder of your puppy, or current keeper of the dog, is feeding. It is unwise to change the diet immediately you get the puppy or dog home. He has enough to cope with, settling into a new environment, without the risk of a tummy upset too. Provided you are careful, you can *slowly* change his food if you wish, provided of course that the food you choose will provide the dog, and particularly the puppy, with all his nutritional requirements. Every dog expert has his own particular favourite canine diet and there is now such a vast selection of dog food available that it can be quite confusing for the first time dog owner to know *what* to feed. Fresh, tinned, dried, vacuum packed – the list is endless. All proprietary brands of dog food have to comply with fairly rigid standards, so whichever you choose from the commercial foods, you should know that your dog is getting the right vitamins and minerals needed for healthy growth. Obviously, puppies have different food requirements from adult dogs, so make sure that you feed the proper puppy diet from the food range you choose. If you decide to feed your puppy on fresh meat, you will need to take advice from your veterinary surgeon as to what supplements you should add, to ensure that your puppy's nutritional requirements are fulfilled.

When deciding what to feed your dog, it is as well to bear in mind what the dog in the wild would have eaten. Their teeth and stomachs were 'designed' to eat fresh meat, grasses, herbs, vegetables and fruit. Dogs have since been domesticated, but the basics remain the same – they still have the sharp canine teeth (the fangs) for ripping flesh, and their stomachs can still digest raw meat. The domestic dog will still enjoy, and benefit from, small quantities of vegetables. Carrots can be fed raw, but others such as potatoes, runner beans and so on should be fed cooked. It is probably best to avoid such things as cabbage and sprouts, as they tend to give dogs the same problems they can give humans! Also, on a serious note, if you feed the dog anything which could cause a build-up of gases in the stomach, you could end up with the dog suffering gastric dilation, which can sometimes prove fatal (see also *Keeping your Dog Healthy* page 100).

Dogs also benefit from being fed *small* quantities of fruit, particularly apples. Given as a treat, a small slice of apple is by far a better titbit than many of the proprietary branded dog treats. Dogs cannot digest refined sugar and, as apples contain only natural sugar, they will not cause any digestive problem, cause damage to the teeth or put on unwanted weight.

Titbits
Having mentioned that dogs cannot digest refined sugar, please do not give them biscuits and snack food sold for human consumption. Titbits are really best reserved as a backup for training when you should either use the proprietary branded type, small pieces of apple, or occasionally cheese. Some specialist companies now sell small packs of training treats, often with liver as a base, as dogs tend to find liver extremely appetising. Again, if fed in large quantities, it will upset the dog's digestion, so go carefully.

How to Serve the Food
The answer to this one may seem glaringly obvious, but only small or medium size dogs should eat with their bowl directly

Larger dogs should be fed at shoulder height.

on the floor. Dogs of a Labrador's size and upwards should ideally be fed with their bowl placed in a stand at shoulder height to the dog. This can aid the journey of the food to the dog's stomach, and can help to avoid the previously mentioned gastric dilation. Unlike humans, who need to chew food to prompt the digestive juices to start flowing, the dog's digestive juices do not start to work until the food reaches the stomach. Dogs therefore gulp their food down, and as a consequence take in large amounts of air as they eat. With the larger dog, if he is fed directly from the floor, the food has to travel upwards first, before passing down into the dog's stomach, so even more air is taken in to assist the food on its journey.

For the same reasons, it is always best to feed your adult dog twice a day, rather than one huge meal. Puppies of course will be fed from between four and six meals a day to begin with.

Preparing the House and Garden
Before the dog or puppy comes home, have a close look at possible dangers around your home and outside in the garden. Make sure that any electrical wires are well tucked away, with nothing showing which a pup could either get caught up in, or pull down. Waste paper bins should be put away from dog height, and shoes should be tidied away. Get into that routine NOW, so that it is automatic by the time the puppy arrives. Get the children into the habit of keeping their bedroom doors closed too. If the children are used to leaving bags of crisps lying around, try and re-train them in advance of the dog's arrival.

Check the fences in the garden. Depending on the size of your dog, make sure that fences and walls will keep him in, not only from a height viewpoint, but also along the bottom of the fence: are there any small holes which the dog could squeeze through? Make sure that the dustbins are either shut away from access, or have properly fitting lids. Check carefully that any chemicals or fertilisers are locked safely away from inquisitive noses. If you have previously used such things as slug pellets in the garden, make sure that all traces are removed – they could kill your puppy. Protect any special shrubs or plants by fencing them off – puppies love to dig!

You can prepare a special area – a digging pit – where you can encourage the dog to dig, to protect those areas where you don't want him to. Choose the spot, about four foot by four foot, dig it over, clear stones etc., maybe add some new soil to the area. Then bury a few suitable toys. When the puppy first goes into the garden, and after he has relieved himself, guide him to the digging pit, and start encouraging him to find the hidden toys, by digging with your hands and saying things like "what's this?" and "where is it?". It won't be long before the pup is scrabbling away with his paws, and when he finds the hidden toy, the reward will be enough to encourage him to dig again. If he is always encouraged to go to the digging pit, and discouraged by fences etc. from the rest of the garden, you should be able to maintain the garden and keep the puppy happy at the same time!

Finally, don't forget to tell your neighbours about the soon to be new arrival. If you warn them in advance that the dog may initially bark or howl at night time, for example, it is less likely that you will have complaints from the neighbours later.

Choosing a Veterinary Surgeon

It is advisable to register with a veterinary surgeon before you bring your puppy home, just in case an emergency should arise where you will need a vet quickly. Take some time and ask other pet owners about their vet, so that you can get an idea which vet will suit you. Obviously, it is more convenient if you choose a practice fairly close to where you live, but it is important that you like the person who is going to be treating your dog, so perhaps you may decide on a practice a little further away, simply because you feel more able to communicate with that particular vet. Ideally, it would be nice if you could go and visit the practice and inspect the areas where your dog or puppy may be treated, such as the kennels and operating theatres. However, bear in mind that veterinary surgeries are busy places, regularly treating very sick animals, and it is therefore unlikely that the staff will be able to spare the time to show you around. Plus, the disturbance to patients, and the risk of bringing infection into the treatment areas, will probably make such a visit impractical. Don't assume that they have 'something to hide' simply because the practice will not allow you to look behind the scenes. Remember, it is possible that at some time during your dog's life, he could be the one who is disturbed, or put at risk, by potential clients 'wanting to view'!

5

BRINGING THE NEW PUPPY OR DOG HOME

Travel Arrangements
It is best if you can arrange to collect the dog early in the day, so that you have as much time as possible with him before you have to settle him down for the first night away from either his mum and his siblings or, if you're getting a dog from a rescue centre, from the place which has meant security to the dog. Take a suitably-sized cardboard box, with a soft warm blanket, for a puppy to travel home in. Alternatively, you may want him to travel on someone's lap – if so, the person holding the puppy should not travel in the front seat. You should take towels, paper towels and plastic bags in case the puppy should have an upset stomach during the journey. Also, a container with fresh drinking water, plus a plastic bowl. Don't feed the puppy during the journey, or you will definitely be using the towels and plastic bags! The breeder should ensure that the puppy is fed well in advance of your arrival, so that the meal will have been digested before the journey. The same applies to adult dogs – the journey may upset them, and any undigested food in their stomach will not stay there long!

Paperwork from the Breeder
Before you leave the breeder, check that you have the pedigree for your puppy (if appropriate), diet sheet, and information on

how often your puppy has been wormed. If you are buying a pedigree puppy, the breeder should have registered the litter with the Kennel Club. You can expect to receive a transfer of ownership form, which you will need to send to the Kennel Club to re-register the puppy in your name, if not at the time you collect your puppy, then fairly soon afterwards, so make sure that it is all in hand before you leave for home.

Arriving Home

With a puppy, carry him in and take him straight through the house into the garden. He will undoubtedly be bursting to go to the toilet, and it will give you your first opportunity to start on the pup's house-training. Reward him when he does relieve himself and allow him to investigate his outside surroundings.

The adult dog will not need to be carried, but again he should be immediately taken to the garden, to establish from the beginning where he is allowed to relieve himself, and to prevent any accidents indoors on his first day.

The puppy will probably be quite tired after the journey, so, having already established where he will sleep, introduce him to his bed and allow him to rest. He may well simply flop onto any available floor space, but do make sure that he can rest without interruption from the children. Visitors to see the puppy should be put off until at least the next day, so that the puppy can settle.

The First Night

With puppies, it is quite natural for them to be a little restless on the first night in your home. Having already decided where the puppy is to sleep, and ensured that he has been fed and been to the toilet, you have to be a little hard-hearted when you hear the first little whine or bark. How you react now will set the pattern for the future. It is a normal human response to want to comfort the puppy, as you will feel sorry for him. What you MUST do, from now on, is think how the dog views *your* actions. If crying or barking provokes you into giving the puppy attention – however understandable it may be for you to want to reassure the puppy – he will view such attention as a reward for his action, that is, crying, whining or barking gets the humans to come to me. Yes, you'll feel rotten and perhaps guilty about ignoring the crying, but the puppy will settle eventually – sometimes within a few minutes, sometimes it may take longer. As each night goes by, you will find that the whining will get less and less, provided you are STRONG!

You can expect to be getting up earlier in the morning for a while! Usually, in the summer, as soon as it is light outside, or in the winter at the first sound the puppy hears, he will be awake and needing to spend a penny. As the puppy grows, you will find that he will sleep later (much like a baby), but in the early days, you should consider anything longer than five or six hours' sleep a positive bonus!

The First Few Days
With any new dog in the house, and particularly with a new puppy, you can expect the first few days to be quite exhausting, but nonetheless very satisfying. Everything which the puppy does will be a learning experience for you and him. Now is the time when you establish the ground rules, for both puppy and adult dog. Don't make the common mistake that so many new owners make, of letting the new dog do things now that you will not want, or accept, in the future. Letting a puppy 'get away' with behaviour because "he's only a baby" will mean that your puppy, when grown into an adult dog, will still expect to be able to continue with that behaviour. If you are homing an adult dog, especially if the dog has had a bad time before you took him, your pity for him may tempt you to spoil him, perhaps by letting him sleep on the furniture, or sleeping on your bed. Dogs are opportunists, and if they are given privileges without really earning them, they will very quickly take over the role of boss, sometimes without you even realising what is happening.

Don't immediately give the dog or puppy access to the entire house. Keep doors closed, or, if your house is open plan, gate off areas that you don't want the dog in. In the dog pack, only the top dog has access to all areas of the "den". The dog sees your house as the den, and by your restricting his access to it, he will quickly understand that he is not the top dog – the humans must be because they can go everywhere, whereas his access is limited (see also *Rank Structuring*, page 53).

Visiting the Vet

Your new puppy will need to see your veterinary surgeon, for a general health check and for the first of his vital preventative vaccinations against distemper, hepatitis, leptospirosis, para influenza and parvo virus. The first vaccination will be given at eight to ten weeks of age, with the second at twelve weeks old. Your puppy should not mix with other dogs, or walk on the ground outside your house and garden until a week to ten days after the second vaccination. You will also need to obtain worming treatment for the puppy. The breeder of your puppy should already have started the worming procedure, and it needs to be continued until the puppy is six months old, and then every six months after that. At that first visit, the vet will tell you at what age your puppy can be given his first treatment for the prevention of fleas. Even if your dog is an adult, it is as well to let your vet check him over, and the adult dog will still need both worm and flea prevention treatment.

Accompanying you and the new puppy or adult dog to the vet is a good way to start educating your children in caring for the new pet. However, please make sure that your children do not cause a nuisance to or disturb other clients and their animals. Many of the dogs, cats or other pets at the surgery will be either feeling unwell, or nervous, or both, and to have noisy children "in their faces" simply adds to their discomfort, as well as possibly causing them to act out of character. The owners of these animals may also be feeling tense and worried, and so may not feel very tolerant of misbehaving children. Ensure that your children are aware of the situation, and that they will sit quietly without trying to stroke or talk to the other animals in the waiting room.

Microchip Identification

During your first trip to the vet, you can find out about micro-chipping your puppy. Micro-chipping is a permanent means of linking your dog to you. A small 'chip', about the size of a grain of rice, is injected between the dog's shoulder blades. It does not go right into the dog, but sits just under the skin. Each chip has an individual number which is recorded against your details and these details are held at a central base. The chip can be read by a small reader, much like the TV remote control. Many vets and most rescue centres have a reader, which they can then use to identify your dog if he is taken to them after being lost or straying.

If you have obtained your dog or puppy from a rescue centre, you may well find that the dog has already been micro-chipped, as many of them now provide that service before the dog goes to his new home.

Even if you have your dog micro-chipped, it is still a legal requirement that he has a visible means of identification. A small disc, with *your* name and a contact number and/or address etched onto it, should be attached to his collar.

Routine
It is important that you quickly establish a regular routine for the new dog or puppy. Sleeping, eating, playing and exercise (once the pup is able to go out) should all happen at around the same time every day. The children should be made to understand that the puppy is not always available to play with, and needs regular rest periods. The older dog will also need periods of quiet.

Visitors
Family and friends will obviously want to come and see the new puppy, but encourage them to come at a time when the puppy would be having a playtime, rather than disturbing a much needed rest period. It is also important that visitors know how to greet the new puppy. It is human nature to want to cuddle the puppy as soon as they arrive at the front door, but if you want to avoid problems in the future, it is best to establish from the start where the puppy is to be greeted, and the front door is not the best place! Most importantly, it could be extremely dangerous, as the puppy could get out. Holding the puppy back, or picking

him up is not the answer either. Whilst you want the puppy to be sociable, if visitors are allowed to pet and give attention to the puppy as soon as they walk in the door, you have the potential for the dog becoming incredibly spoiled, getting everything he asks for and being a pain to live with! You do not want your puppy to think that he is the most important member of the household, which he soon will if every new person who visits the house gives him attention immediately, almost before stepping over the threshold.

Establish from the beginning that when visitors arrive, the puppy should remain in the kitchen. The visitors can then be invited into the house safely, without risk to the puppy from an open front door. Then bring the visitors into the kitchen, but ask them not to immediately fall onto their knees to say hello to the pup. If the puppy is leaping around, trying to get attention, ask the visitors to ignore him. Settle the visitors, perhaps at the kitchen table, and, once the puppy has stopped trying to get their attention, invite them to say hello to the puppy. It is difficult, I know, for people to ignore a cuddly bundle of puppy, but it will be worth it in the long run. If you start off this way, you will avoid a situation which many people will recognise – that of having a dog "in your face" as soon as you step into the house. The pup will quickly learn two things – he is not greeted at the front door, so will be more likely to take himself into the kitchen where he knows he will be petted, and also that the way to get attention is not to demand it!

6

THE FIRST FEW MONTHS

Over the next few weeks, it is vital that you show the dog, in a logical way, where he fits within the family group. Today, more and more owners are consulting dog behaviourists because the dog is exhibiting behaviour which they don't like, even whilst the dog is still just a few months old. The most common reason why unacceptable behaviour develops is that the dog is acting like a dog, and the owner tries to apply human logic to the problem, rather than understanding how the dog interprets *our* behaviour.

Inconsistent Behaviour
As an example, on a nice dry sunny day, the dog comes in from the garden and is allowed straight through into the rest of the house. On a wet day, when the dog will have wet and muddy feet, in he comes, attempts to continue his usual pattern of going into the rest of the house, and, because we don't want muddy paw marks on the carpet, we shout and scream, perhaps slamming the door in his face. To us, this is very logical, but to the dog, who doesn't have any understanding of the difference between dirty carpet and clean carpet, he sees our behaviour as unpredictable – one day he is allowed in the entire house, the next he is told off for repeating the same routine.

We confuse dogs with our inconsistencies – at home we play with them on the floor, we make ''baby'' sounds at them in a soft and loving voice. Outside in the park, where people may be watching and we don't want to be thought of as soft, we don't play with them, don't talk lovingly to them – indeed we may be rather gruff voiced. We try to be leader of the pack, but when our dog tries to initiate a ''pack'' hunt, and rolls in the droppings of the animal to be hunted, like fox or deer, we get very cross, shouting and rushing at him to stop doing it.

At home, we may encourage them to climb on our lap, or jump up at us for a welcome or a cuddle. When visitors call and the dog attempts to repeat the same, previously encouraged behaviour with the visitor, we are embarrassed, and tell him to get off. We may accidentally drop some human food onto the floor and call the dog to come and clean it up – we then get cross when the dog attempts to eat the same smelling food from the kitchen work top!

All these examples – and there are many more – completely confuse the dog. We must therefore look at how our actions are interpreted by the dog, and NOT attribute the dog with human values. If we don't, mistrust and misunderstanding are built up, seriously affecting our ability to train our dogs.

Lifestyles
The way dogs are kept today is very different from when I was a child. Then, the dog was either kept outside in a kennel, or at least confined to the kitchen. Very occasionally the dog was allowed into the living accommodation, and he was *never* allowed upstairs. Because homes were not centrally heated, doors were kept closed to retain heat, and therefore the dog was not given access to the rest of the house – only by special invitation. Now, whilst that is certainly not the way I like to keep my dogs, what it did demonstrate very clearly to the dog was his position within the household. The humans had access to all areas, whereas he was only allowed in certain areas – his understanding of that situation was that he was lower in rank than the humans. As a result, the dog, knowing his position, did not attempt to 'take rank', nor try and dominate with shows of aggression or attention-seeking behaviour.

With more people going out to work full-time, many dogs are left alone for up to eight hours a day. Dogs are naturally gregarious – they need company – and left alone for hours on end they become bored, stressed and destructive. When the owners come home in the evening, the dog is so thrilled with having company that he gets over-excited, perhaps hyper-active, and the owners just can't cope with the attention which the dog is naturally demanding. Walking the dog becomes a chore which has to be fitted into an already hectic life, rather than an enjoyable time for dog and owner to interact.

Often, the first thing the owner does when returning home from work is to feed the dog – perhaps because of guilt at having left the dog alone. It may be that he or she wants to get the feeding 'out of the way', so as to concentrate on preparing the family meal. No matter what the reason, the dog views his feeding as being more important than the human's, because he is fed first. His pack understanding tells him that the most important member of the pack eats first.

Years ago, only a few households had access to a car, so the dog was walked everywhere, satisfying two very important needs – *socialising*, by meeting people and encountering different situations (perhaps on the daily walk to school with the children), and *exercise*, stimulating and enjoyable time spent bonding with the family. Nowadays, the dog tends to travel to the park by car and the children travel to school by car, so the dog's world is reduced considerably, limiting both mental and physical exercise.

Rank Structuring
Having touched on this subject in the section covering the first few days (page 47), there are procedures which you can implement to ensure that your dog understands where he fits within your family group. Not all of the suggestions have to be carried on forever, but simply put in place until your dog is at a level which is acceptable to you and the family.

1. Confine the dog to one room in the house for a few minutes every day. This is not meant as a punishment, so don't be gruff or unkind when you shut him away. This simply shows the dog that he cannot always be with you

or follow you around. Ignore barking and whining and scratching at the door, and don't let him out whilst he is making a noise.

Don't allow your dog to occupy key areas in the house.

2. Don't allow him to occupy key areas in the house – doorways and the top of the stairs are all areas that should be controlled by the leader of the pack, and if your dog sees himself as higher ranked, he will feel it is his place to control these areas. Height especially is associated with rank. Your bed, or on the furniture, and as already mentioned, the top of the stairs, are all important areas to the dog to take or maintain his position of rank. Make these areas inaccessible to the dog – put a stair gate across the bottom of the stairs, keep bedroom doors closed and deny access to furniture. Tip up chairs in the lounge, or cover the seats with kitchen foil (dogs do not like the sound or feel of foil under their feet). Block access to the settee.

3. For a few minutes every day, for a couple of weeks, sit in the dog's bed or den! Make sure the dog can see you.

Yes, you'll feel very silly, but it is important for you to show the dog that you can occupy any area, and that he does not have 'ownership' or right over any place or thing – the bed is yours, and you allow him to use it!

4. Eat before the dog does. The dog understands that higher ranked individuals eat first. If your meal times do not coincide with the dog's, then at least have a snack or eat a biscuit before you put the dog's food down for him to eat.

5. Always make the dog move out of your way, never step over or walk around him. Again, the dog's understanding is that lower ranked individuals have to make way for those with higher rank.

6. Don't succumb to demands for attention. Dogs learn to do this in many ways – nudging your arm for a stroke, pawing at you, jumping up, continually bringing toys to you. Any contact should always be instigated by you, and then earned by getting the dog to do something for you first – a simple sit is enough – before you give him a fuss.

7. Toys. The dog should have access to toys when he is left alone, but when you are in the house toys should only be made available when you are going to play with the dog. You want the dog to understand that they are *your* toys (as a lower ranked individual he has access to nothing, unless you give him permission). Select a toy, have a game and then take back possession of the toy. Some dogs, even very young puppies, can display aggressive signs with tug-of-war games – try to avoid this type of toy, and do not let the children play tuggy games with the dog.

8. Always insist that you go through a doorway first, and don't allow the dog to barge past you.

9. Every day, have a light training session with the dog for a few minutes – sit, down and stand, and eventually stay. This will not only help the dog to learn these basic exercises, but it again gives you the opportunity of some quality bonding time with him.

As the dog accepts his position within the family, you may wish to introduce more privileges and allow the dog more access to the family areas. Provided the dog does not take advantage and view these privileges as a sign of your weakness, there is no harm in bringing the dog to a level at which *you* are happy. Some people do not mind their dogs being on the furniture, for example, but it is so important that your dog understands that you are giving him that access, as opposed to him taking it.

House-training

Puppies
One of the first routines to be established with any new puppy, and perhaps with some adult dogs, is where and when it is appropriate to relieve himself. Please accept that there will be some accidents indoors, and please DO NOT punish the puppy or even the adult dog for these accidents.

Going to the toilet is a normal bodily function, and as far as a dog is concerned, especially a puppy, when they need to go, they go where they happen to be! The fact that the 'delivery' of either urine or faeces on the carpet is obnoxious to us is a concept that dogs do not understand. The 'old wives tale' of rubbing the dog's nose in the mess (ugh!) or throwing the puppy outside, so they will learn that it is wrong, is completely misguided. The fact that puppies treated in such a manner do eventually become house-trained is more luck than anything else – they would have become house-trained anyway. What such treatment *does* do is build up mistrust between human and dog, as in the dog's mind, such behaviour is illogical and makes humans even more difficult to understand.

Bearing in mind that the puppy will need to go to the toilet frequently, it is up to you to ensure that when that need arises, the puppy is in an appropriate place to perform the required action. As such, take the puppy into the garden as soon as he wakes from sleeping, as soon as he has eaten, after a playtime, and every hour apart from that! The need to visit the garden will reduce as the number of mealtimes is reduced – remember that at seven weeks old your puppy may be having up to six meals per day, which will gradually be reduced to two by the time he is about six months old.

Note that I said TAKE the puppy into the garden – if you simply put him outside unsupervised, he may go to the toilet, or he may simply play and sniff, quickly forgetting what he is out there to do. This could well result in him coming indoors and peeing on the carpet! If you are not outside with him to reward him, he will not learn that going to the toilet outside pleases you, whereas when he performs the same action indoors, it gets ignored. If you use small food treats for rewarding him outside as soon as he 'empties', at the same time using a simple sound, like "be quick" or "hurry up", you will quickly be able to get him to go to the toilet on command, as he will associate that sound with his action, plus the reward at the end of said action.

To begin with, you may find that you have to stay outside with the puppy for quite a while before he performs the required action. Don't be tempted into a game with the pup, or he will never do what is required. Without losing sight of him, try and ignore him, removing any toys he may bring to you in an attempt to get you to play. Don't get cross or impatient – it may be cold, raining and thundering, but he still needs to go to the toilet.

If you choose to train the puppy to use newspaper indoors to begin with, you will eventually successfully house-train him, but it will take a little longer, as you will have to "de-train" him from the paper first. Unless your puppy is unrestricted at night time, in which case he will have access to the floor, I would suggest that you don't use newspaper indoors.

When the puppy is old enough to go out on exercise, you can continue with the sound he will have learned in the garden, and the puppy will quickly understand where it is appropriate to go to the toilet, rather than embarrass you by going on the pavement – and remember, wherever he does relieve himself outside, don't forget to clean up after him!

Adult Dogs

Sometimes adult dogs will forget their house-training – either through trauma or perhaps because, if they were in a rescue centre, they have spent some time in a kennel environment when they could relieve themselves where they liked. Much of the previous advice on house-training puppies works just as well with the adult dog. It is so important to remember that any 'accidents' are not deliberate, and that the dog is not wrong, just a bit confused because of his new surroundings. Punishment for mistakes on the carpet will simply lead to the dog becoming bewildered at your attitude and perhaps more secretive about where indoors he does his toilet.

Occasionally, a newly re-homed adult male dog will attempt to "territory mark' his new home, by cocking his leg on the corners of furniture, doors and so on, thereby leaving his scent for other dogs to know he is there, and also to reassure himself that his new home smells of him. Again, punishment will not solve the problem. Obviously, ensure that you clean the areas thoroughly and, where possible, move the 'inviting' pieces of furniture to less strategic places. The quickest way to stop this territory marking is to settle the dog into a proper routine immediately, letting the dog know where his boundaries are, and ensuring that at the same time he receives plenty of loving reassurance when he goes to the toilet in the appropriate place.

Training Classes

Puppy Parties

Because early socialising with a new puppy is so important to his mental development, many vets are now running puppy parties at their surgeries. Puppies who are not yet fully vaccinated, and therefore unable to go outside on the ground yet, can interact with other puppies in the clinical environment of the surgery. Whilst the puppies are interacting with each other, their owners receive basic advice on the training and general care of the puppy. The parties are held outside normal consulting hours, and the floor will have been cleaned with an anti-bacterial and virucidal disinfectant. Bearing in mind that the puppies will not have been exposed to external infection, either from the ground or from contact with other dogs, and having been brought straight from home and returning back there afterwards, the risk of infection is extremely low. Puppy to puppy cross-infection is possible, so you will be advised, before attending, not to bring your puppy if he is showing any signs of illness, such as diarrhoea, coughing or scratching.

The advantages of early socialisation far outweigh the very slight risk of infection, so, if your veterinary surgeon offers this service, do make the most of the opportunity.

Dog Training Clubs

As a dog trainer and behaviourist, I am obviously going to recommend that you take your puppy, or your older dog, to classes. Nowadays, with more classes catering for puppies from 13 weeks old and upwards, it is invaluable from the point of view of stopping possible problems before they become a learned behaviour. The puppies also learn basic commands such as "sit", "stay" and "come", all whilst in the company of other puppies, which is what will be expected of your pup when out on exercise. It is all very well teaching your puppy to be obedient whilst in the confines of your own home, but frequently you will find that all his training is forgotten as soon as the puppy meets another dog outside. Going to classes is also a good way of socialising your pup with other like-minded people, who are unlikely to get upset if your puppy jumps up or licks them.

For the adult dog, classes are a good way to build up the bond between you and the dog, as the dog will be taught to obey you, as the new leader of the pack. You will also be able to get help with any problems that may occur, as the dog settles into his new home.

Most veterinary surgeries have details of where training classes are held. Recommendation is often the best way of picking a training club, as by talking to other dog owners you can find the right class for you. Training methods have changed enormously over the years, and most clubs now teach along the lines of positive reinforcement, that is, praising all the good stuff your dog does whilst ignoring any wrong behaviour as much as possible. Classes which use negative reinforcement, that is, punishing the wrong behaviour, are to be avoided. Dogs do not understand our values, and only by praising all the things we like will they learn what pleases us. To punish them when they make a mistake, when in their mind it is not a mistake but normal dog behaviour, only builds up mistrust in their minds, making future training more difficult.

Exercise

If you have re-homed an adult dog, then you can start taking him out immediately, provided he has had all the usual vaccinations. The amount of exercise the dog will need should be appropriate for the size and age of the dog. As mentioned at the beginning, it is wrong to assume that a small dog such as a Jack Russell Terrier will not need as much exercise as a German Shepherd Dog, for example. Obviously, *all* dogs should be taken out *at least* once a day, preferably more, and at least one of those daily walks should be off-the-lead exercise. Depending on the time you have available, all dogs will benefit from at least an hour off-the-lead exercise daily.

With young puppies, once they are allowed out, the exercise should be modified according to the size of dog they will eventually become. A common mistake is for new owners of the larger breeds to assume that the puppies can take more exercise, as they grow so rapidly. With the larger breeds, the puppies *are* growing quickly, and as such their bones can be easily damaged by too much strenuous exercise. The smaller breeds still need to take it carefully to begin with, even though they don't have so much growing to do.

Take advice from both the breeder of your puppy, and from your veterinary surgeon, as to how much exercise your particular puppy should have.

Early Learning

Even assuming that you will be taking your puppy or dog to classes, you will need to start training your dog almost as soon as he enters your home. Most of the following relates to puppies, but will apply equally to the adult dog if he has developed any of the behaviours mentioned.

Grooming and Examining Your Puppy
Whatever type of coat your puppy has, you should start by brushing him daily, so that his coat never gets into a tangled or unkempt state. If that happens, grooming could cause the puppy discomfort, which will not aid his acceptance of the procedure. Even when he still has his 'baby' coat, daily gentle brushing will get him used to accepting that this is a normal part of his life. Obviously, at the start you will be using a soft brush, only progressing to a harder brush and comb when the puppy's adult coat has come through.

Whilst you are brushing, you can check your puppy over, firstly so that you can detect any possible problem that may be developing, and also to teach the puppy to stand still and be examined, as he will have to at the vet. Regularly looking at his teeth, ears, feet, tummy and so on, touching and feeling him all over, as the vet might do, will all help in spotting a potential health problem. If you are used to how the dog looks when he is healthy, you will quickly notice when something is amiss. A puppy who accepts having his ears examined, or having his feet picked up and felt, will be more prepared to be examined by the vet, if and when there is a problem. Your puppy may need his toe nails clipping, for example, and if he has never had his feet touched before, such a procedure will be extremely difficult for your vet to perform.

If you have a male puppy, you should check that he is developing properly – his testicles will be held up inside his body to begin with, and will eventually descend by the time he is an adult dog. Very occasionally the testes become retained inside, which will be a matter for your vet to deal with, so you will need to check regularly to ensure that the puppy is maturing as he should.

If you have a female puppy, she will hopefully be having at least one season first before you have her spayed (see page 94). Bitch puppies come into season any time from five months onwards, and you should know what she looks like around her vaginal area when she *isn't* in season, so that you can spot the difference when she is!

If the idea of checking these basic things is abhorrent to you, then perhaps now is the time to think again about getting a dog!

Cleaning the Dog's Teeth
This should be included in the grooming and examination routine. (See Chapter 9, page 108.)

Jumping Up
When trying to deter or to 'de-train' a dog from any behaviour, it is important to understand the reason for exhibiting this behaviour in the first place. All puppies will try to jump up at you, or your visitors. They do this because they want to get close to our faces and particularly our mouths – a food-soliciting behaviour carried over from when dogs were wild. It can also be dominance related – the dog wants to place his paws on you. Initially, when a puppy jumps up at us our reaction teaches him that we like him doing it. How does that happen? One or more of several things occur which confirms in the dog's mind that he is pleasing us. With little puppies especially, we tend to tolerate the jumping up because they are sweet and appealing, and we feel they need our reassurance all the time. We are also sometimes quietly pleased that the puppy wants our attention. Once we get tired of the puppy jumping at us, we start pushing him off and at the same time talking to him, telling him to get off. Either reaction is pleasant for the puppy – he is either being touched, spoken to, or both. Even if you push the puppy off abruptly, they like to play fight quite roughly, so do not see being pushed off as a deterrent, even seeing it as a game. To the dog, his action has provoked a reaction from you that will prompt a repeat of the behaviour, so he will continue to jump up.

So, to stop him jumping up, you have to change the previous rewarding experience for the dog into an *un*rewarding one. IGNORE the dog completely. Don't touch or speak to him. Turn your back on him, folding your arms so they are not

To stop the dog jumping up, ignore him completely.

accessible for the dog to touch. If he jumps at your back, take a step away from him. Don't acknowledge him in any way all the time he is jumping up at you. When he eventually has four feet on the ground, immediately *go down to his level* and give him a big fuss and a titbit.

Eventually, when you have taught him to sit on command, you can reinforce the control by making him sit as well, but at this stage you simply want him to understand that four feet on the floor get attention, whereas two feet on you don't! If everyone who comes to the house follows the same procedure, the puppy will quickly learn that the way to get attention is to remain on the floor.

Mouthing and Biting – Puppies
All puppies will attempt to mouth and bite their human family. It is perfectly normal behaviour, developed when they are still

with their siblings in the litter. The sharp, needle-like teeth which the puppy has until around 16 to 18 weeks of age are there for a very good reason – to cause pain, but little damage. The jaw muscles are not so strong at that age, and by play fighting with their litter mates, and later with us, these teeth enable them to cause and feel pain.

When playing with their litter brothers and sisters, they learn that, if they bite too hard, the puppy who has been bitten yelps loudly, and then often refuses to continue playing. Likewise, when they are bitten, they yelp and run away from the biter. Thus they learn that biting too hard hurts and stops the fun – an unrewarding experience. The process continues and they learn to modify the biting whilst playing, until a level is reached which the other puppies can tolerate.

The difference when they attempt to repeat that behaviour with us is that we have to show the puppy that we will not tolerate any level of biting. We should use the already learned response when the puppy attempts either to bite or even simply 'hold' our hand in his mouth. A very sharp scream of ''OUCH'', followed immediately by ceasing all contact with the puppy for a few minutes, will prompt the memory learned in the litter. Our 'yelp' will remind him of *his* yelp when he was bitten, and our refusal to play or interact with him will again remind him of how his siblings ceased playing when he bit them.

After the 'time-out' of a couple of minutes, re-establish contact with the puppy. You may find that the pup will attempt to lick you, as a sign of appeasement. If you do not object to the puppy licking you, then as he does so, use the word ''gently'', to show the puppy that this is acceptable, and to begin conditioning him to that sound, which will prompt a repeat of the action. You may find that the puppy will simply try to bite again, probably a little softer this time. If he does, repeat the yelp procedure, until you are able to re-establish contact with him without him attempting to open his mouth on you.

Puppies will repeat behaviour they find rewarding, i.e. a game and contact with you. They will cease behaviour that is unrewarding i.e. mouthing and biting stops the contact.

Mouthing and Biting – Adult Dogs

If you have taken on an adult dog who has not learned properly that biting or mouthing humans is unacceptable, he will sometimes use such behaviour in an attempt to dominate you, to try and take over as pack leader. If allowed to continue, it may eventually lead to the dog biting seriously, causing damage. Your reaction to this behaviour from an adult dog is very different from that used on a puppy.

Any attempt to take hold of your hand, or clothing, should be met with a loud "GET OFF", and glaring eye contact. Don't shout or scream, simply adopt the attitude of "how dare you do that to the boss of the pack". DON'T reward him by saying "good boy" when he stops. A dog should not be rewarded for stopping behaviour that he shouldn't have been doing in the first place! When the dog has stopped, reinforce your mental dominance by ordering the dog to do something for you, however small. Tell him to sit, or lie down. When he has completed that action for you, you can *then* reward him for compliance, showing him the type of behaviour which you will accept and praise him for.

Chewing and Destructiveness

If you follow the earlier suggestion of having an indoor kennel for your puppy, you will find that you will not have much of a problem in the chewing department. Providing the puppy with something appropriate to chew on when he is teething will also deter him from chewing on furniture and so on. Occasionally, the dog may go through a second chewing stage, between six to nine months, as the new adult teeth are settling into the jaw bone. Again, suitable chew toys given at that time will save your furniture.

Incorrect diet can sometimes be a contributory factor in chewing, especially if the diet is lacking in fibre. Door frames and wooden furniture then become a replacement for the missing element of the diet. A check with your vet may be needed, who will be able to suggest a possible diet change to solve this particular problem.

Lack of exercise and mental stimulation can also create the need for the dog to relieve the boredom by chewing. Most of the damage done by chewing usually occurs whilst you are out of the house. Please remember that chewing or destroying your home is NOT done out of spite. The act of chewing is self-rewarding, either by easing the aching teeth, chewing something which smells of you if the puppy is lonely, or employing the 'killing' instinct by shredding your settee!

By ensuring that the puppy is safely contained away from the furniture, has suitable toys to stimulate his brain, has something he can demolish, and has been played with and/or exercised before being left alone, you will be able to control this aspect of your puppy's development to within an acceptable level.

Mounting – Puppies
Please don't be horrified if your puppy of just a couple of months old attempts to mount you or the children! Both male and female puppies experiment by mounting, either each other or a human. It does not mean that the puppy is perverted. Gently guide the puppy away, and distract him or her with a toy. Sometimes it may be a sign that the puppy is trying to be dominant, but again this should be dealt with in the same way – gentle distraction. If you play down the behaviour, it will cease to be rewarding for the puppy and he or she will grow out of it before reaching adulthood.

Mounting – Adult Dogs
Adult dogs who try to mount are nearly always trying to dominate their human family. Castration for the males, and spaying for the females, will usually sort this problem out, along with some remedial rank re-structuring.

Leaving the Puppy Alone
All dogs have to be left alone sometimes, and the puppy will have to learn that there will be regular periods when you go out without him. You will need to slowly acclimatise him to being

left, starting with just a few minutes and building up to longer periods over the weeks and months ahead.

To begin with, get the puppy used to being left in one room whilst you are in another, just for a couple of minutes. Yet again, the indoor kennel is invaluable here, enabling you simply to put him into his kennel and close the door, which prevents him from being able to follow you. Leave the room and close the door behind you. You don't have to creep about trying to be quiet – you want the pup just to get used to the idea that he doesn't always follow you.

Within a few days, you should easily be able to leave the puppy alone in one room for at least half an hour. Once you have reached that goal, you can now begin to leave him in that room whilst you go out, to begin with for no longer than fifteen minutes. Always make sure that the puppy has been outside to go to the toilet first, and has suitable toys to amuse him whilst you are out. Again, over a period of a few days, you should be able to build up the period of being left to about one hour.

Ideally, no dog should be left for more than 3 hours at a time. If you have to leave him for longer periods, you should arrange for someone to come in after a couple of hours, to let the puppy into the garden, and to give the puppy some company for a while.

Leaving Adult Dogs Alone

Hopefully, the adult dog you have brought into your home has already learned that at times he has to remain alone. There are some dogs, though, who have become anxious about being left and will chew and demolish everything they can lay their teeth on, howl or bark, soil indoors and even sometimes self mutilate, the whole time you are out. For these dogs, being left is almost like being punished. They find it particularly stressful as they don't understand what they may have done to receive such treatment from you. Dogs who have already had several homes may be particularly affected by being left. Quite simply, because they have already 'lost' previous owners, when you leave them to go out, they don't know if you're coming back or if they have been deserted once again. When you are at home, the dog may follow you from room to room, even to the bathroom. He may always want to sit at your feet, perhaps with one of his paws on your foot. He may object when a door is accidentally closed on him. All these are signs that the dog is suffering from what is called 'separation anxiety'.

This problem can be sorted out, although it is a slow process. To begin with, shut the dog in a room on his own for just fifteen seconds. When you put him in the room, be very cool, not cross, but just leave him in there without saying anything. Leave an article of your clothing laying across the bottom of the outside of the door. That way, when he sits and sniffs at the door, he will be able to smell you, which will reassure him. Leave a radio on in the room with him, and an interesting toy to play with. Don't be tempted to try for longer than fifteen seconds to start with.

When he can be left for that length of time without scratching at the door, or barking or howling, start building up the time until you can leave him for ten minutes. You can then start preparing to leave the dog when you go out. Make sure he has had a good walk before you go. Leaving him with a full stomach will encourage the dog to rest. Up until this time, you will have probably found that the dog begins to get worried long before you actually leave him, following you about and initiating contact with you whenever he can. This is because he 'picks up the signals' that you are going out, as your routine is always the same. That routine culminates in you perhaps putting on your coat, or picking up your keys, then giving the dog a cuddle, to reassure him.

What you need to do is completely to change your leaving routine, so that the dog cannot pick up on the leaving signals. Reduce contact with the dog at least an hour before you go out. You don't need to be cross with him, just don't talk to or touch him. If he tries to initiate contact with you, ignore him. When it is time to leave, just walk out, saying nothing to the dog. By following this procedure, you are slowly withdrawing from the closeness which has previously been present up until the moment you leave. One minute, the dog has been in warm contact with you, and the next, you're gone, leaving him bereft. By slowly reducing that contact prior to leaving, the act of you going is not nearly so stressful for the dog. When you return, you can greet the dog lovingly as usual – even if you find he has destroyed something whilst you have been out!

If you are cross with him when you come home, he does not know that it is because he has chewed something precious. All he learns is that you are angry when you return, and probably best avoided. The next time you return home, it is likely the dog will be even more stressed, as he will be anticipating your grumpy return. As such, the stress he feels may well culminate in even more damage being done, and thus the circle of destruction continues!

Car Travel

Cars are now an integral part of our lives and as such will also become a necessary part of your dog's routine. Bear in mind that, if you have a puppy, his first experience of a car was when he left his natural mother and siblings, so the initial introduction to the car may have left the puppy with an unpleasant and unhappy association. The very next car ride he experienced was probably a trip to the vet for his first inoculations, so it is hardly surprising that many young dogs develop travel sickness – to him it quickly becomes a signal of something stressful about to happen.

To change the dog's attitude about the car, make sure that pleasant things happen there – for a week or two feed him one of his daily meals in the car, whilst it is parked outside. Take the time every day and go and sit with him in the car, without the engine running. Have the car radio on and, assuming that he is not showing fear or misapprehension, spend the time talking to and stroking him. If he is shaking, whining or showing any fearful behaviour, *do not initiate or allow any contact*. Touching or talking to the dog whilst he is exhibiting such behaviour will simply re-affirm in his mind that such behaviour is appropriate in that situation, as you are rewarding him for it. Only reward (by touching and talking) behaviour that is non-fearful.

Even before he can go out on the ground and mix with other dogs, take him out for short rides in the car to visit friends or family who will make a fuss of him. Dogs will usually travel better in the car if they are confined in one area. If you have an estate car you can buy purpose-made cages which will fit in the rear of the car. With a saloon car, either tie the lead to a strong part of the inside of the car (not the door handle!), or buy a proper dog safety harness, which can be attached securely, preventing the dog from charging about in the car, and just as importantly protecting the dog and the front seat passenger in the event of a traffic accident.

A safety harness prevents your dog from charging about the car.

7

TRAINING

You will obviously need to teach your dog the basic obedience required to ensure that he doesn't cause a nuisance to other people, is controlled enough to run freely and safely when out on exercise, and is a pleasure to own.

Hopefully, you will be taking him to classes to complete his formal education, where you can get advice and instruction in the art of getting him to walk nicely on a lead, sitting and lying down on command, staying when told and coming when called. More advanced training is available (see *Obedience Competitions*, page 88), but in terms of the control you will need for a family pet, the following will be quite sufficient to start with.

Sitting on Command
This is usually the very first exercise that we teach our dogs and is what I describe in my classes as "gears in neutral, hand brake on"! In other words, the 'sit' tends to be used to get the dog's attention before something else happens, i.e. sitting before being petted by visitors, sitting before being fed, or sitting before having the lead put on, or taken off. Most owners manage to teach the dog to sit for a few moments before he gets up of his own accord, but what you want to achieve is the dog sitting *until he is told he can move*.

To begin teaching the sit, you don't need to have the dog on a lead, and it doesn't matter if the dog is in front of you or by your side. What is crucial is titbits! Many people seem to think that if you use titbits for training, the dog will never do anything without them, but here we will use titbits as an initial 'lure', whilst at the same time teaching the dog a voice signal and a hand signal which are going to mean 'sit'. Eventually the titbits will be phased right down, only being given occasionally, but to start with you will be using them all the time.

Again, many people would begin to teach the dog to sit by saying the word "sit", at the same time pushing down on the dog's rump, until he sits. There is a better way! You want the dog to work out what he has to do to get the titbit. In other words, he has to use his brain. If he uses his brain, rather than being pushed or shoved into a position, he will *remember*.

Have plenty of titbits in your pocket, with one or two in your hand. With the palm of your hand facing *upwards*, and holding a titbit between your first three fingers and thumb, 'waft' the titbit in front of the dog's nose, then straight up about three inches directly above his nose, and hold it there. Say nothing. He may just stand there, trying to work out what it is he has to do. He may offer several different 'behaviours' in an attempt to get the titbit. He may bark – ignore it. He may attempt to jump up at your hand – just lower your hand to under the dog's head momentarily and he will stop jumping.

The mere fact that the dog can smell the titbit will make him tip his nose up towards it. As his nose tips up, his back end will dip down and he will sit. As he sits, say the words "good SIT" dropping your hand to the level of his mouth and offer him the titbit, *without letting go of it*. Let him nibble on it whilst you are still holding it, all the time saying, "What a good SIT, clever SIT", and continue to reward the dog all the time he remains sitting.

You should continue to re-enforce the sound of SIT all the time he is sitting – building up a sound to go with his action, so that he will learn the command. Keep him in the sit position, allowing him to nibble on the titbit, for about five seconds, then, as you release the titbit completely, say "that'll do", and allow the dog to move. You will find that once the titbit has been handed over, the dog will move almost immediately. By using the "that'll do" command, you will teach

"SIT".

the dog that, as those words are said, he can move.

If the dog attempts to move from the sit whilst he is still nibbling on the titbit you are holding, just move your hand up slightly, then reposition it just above the dog's nose, as you did initially, and he will sit again.

Once he is sitting immediately your hand goes up in front of his nose, you can start to use the command of "sit" before he sits – in other words, giving him the command to do the action. You will find that the dog will 'pick up' on the hand signal too – as your hand raises, so he will start to sit. He is therefore learning both signals – voice and hand – which is very useful if the dog's hearing deteriorates when he is older, as you will still be able to 'tell' him to sit with your hand, even if he can't hear your voice. It's also useful if you lose your voice too!

As soon as he is sitting happily on either the verbal or visual command, or both, you can begin to get the dog to accept sitting for you either in front of you, or at your side. Using the titbit as a lure again, you can guide the dog around until he is sitting adjacent to your leg.

Lying Down on Command

"DOWN".

In the same way that you teach the sit, the down is taught with titbits initially, backed up with a hand signal. To begin with, do not say anything until the dog offers the correct behaviour, that is, he lies down. The dog should be sitting before you start the exercise – eventually you will be able to get him to lie down from the standing position, but to begin with it is easier for both of you if he is sitting. Again, you need two or three titbits in your hand, held slightly under your fingers with your thumb, but this time you hold your hand *palm downwards*. Start with your hand adjacent to and immediately in front of the dog's nose, and take your hand directly down until your hand is resting on the floor, ending up in the middle of the space between the dog's front paws and directly below his nose. Keep your hand still. The dog will probably just tip his head downwards to begin with, without lying down. He may scratch at your hand with his paw. Ignore it, and if necessary slightly move your hand to avoid his paw. He may stand up from the sit position – if he does, simply repeat the sit, reward him verbally for sitting, but don't give him a titbit for sitting this time, as on this occasion he has to earn the titbit by lying down. He may bark – ignore it. Don't be tempted into saying anything. You want the dog to work out for himself just what he has to do to get the titbit. Some dogs seem to get the hang of this very quickly, and will lie down within a few seconds. Others may take several minutes for the penny to drop. You will know when the dog is getting an inkling of what to do when he not only tips his head down to your hand, but he slightly bends his front legs. When this happens, *slowly* slide your hand about four to six inches out from his nose, without moving your hand from the floor. As his nose follows your hand, so his shoulders will bend and he will be lying down. The second his shoulders touch the floor, give him the titbit *without letting go* and tell him "good DOWN, clever DOWN". Allow him to nibble on the titbit for a few seconds whilst he is still lying down, then give it to him, saying, "that'll do", and allowing him to move.

Walking on the Lead

Walking correctly.

A dog who pulls continually is not a pleasure to take out. You may be lucky in getting one of those rare animals who doesn't try and pull, but most dogs will try and 'take the lead', usually because they want to take control as leader of the "hunt", as that is how a dog perceives going for a walk with his owner.

Most novice owners make the mistake of trying to pull the dog back each time he pulls forward. What then happens is a battle not only of wills, but strength too. As a dog has four feet to your two, and as his centre of gravity is lower than yours, he will usually win! A dog will automatically pull against pressure – pressure invites counter pressure – so you will see that the way to teach him to walk nicely is not to get into that particular battle in the first place!

What you want to aim for is the dog walking nicely on a loose lead, not 'glued' to your leg, but without continually trying to take up the slack. He is allowed to walk slightly in front of you, provided he is not pulling. Walking to heel, really close to your leg, is not what we're aiming at here – that can come later. You can also teach this without putting any special collar around the dog's neck – again, for more precise work, you may do well to purchase a double action check collar – NOT A CHOKE CHAIN – but for now, a normal flat leather collar will suffice, together with a leather or nylon lead, about three or four feet long.

A normal flat, leather collar, together with a leather or nylon lead, will suffice.

Don't try teaching the dog not to pull when you're on the way out for the first walk of the day. The dog will be so excited at going out that you will have a hard task on your hands just to get him to pay attention, let alone not to pull. The best place to begin teaching the dog is in the garden. Attach the lead to the dog's collar and *stand still*. Make up your mind now which side the dog is going to walk on – left or right – and stick to it. You don't want the dog to be continually swapping sides in front of you. Hold the lead with both hands close together, at the end of the lead. Have a few titbits in one hand. If the dog makes no attempt to pull, tell him "good STEADY", and give him a titbit. All the time he makes no attempt to pull, keep verbally rewarding him. *Keep standing still.* When he makes the first effort to pull and take up the slack of the lead, give a *little gentle* flick on the lead, so that it momentarily tightens, and then release the tension so that the lead goes slack again. *Keep standing still.* As you flick the lead, give the command 'steady'. The flick will have the effect of slightly unbalancing the dog, which will make him turn and look at you, having the effect of slackening the lead. Reward the dog for both looking at you and taking the pressure off.

Repeat the flick of the lead each time the dog attempts to take up the slack, and reward him each time he responds to the flick and "steady" word. Make sure that there is obvious slack in the lead between each flick. Don't rush the procedure, and don't be tempted to walk yet – keep still. Don't worry if the dog decides to sit – just take a couple of steps backwards to get him up on his feet.

When the dog is happy to stand, with the lead slack, for about ten seconds (count it out under your breath), take one step forward. If the dog tries to pull again, stand still immediately and flick the lead again, using the 'steady' command. Make it clear to the dog that, if he pulls, you stand still, and after each attempt and correction, ensure the dog realises what has happened before you attempt another step forward.

For this first lesson, you want to aim for about ten paces without the dog pulling. Walk at a speed which is comfortable for you and don't allow the dog to dictate how fast you go. All the time the dog is walking without taking up the slack of the lead, tell him what a clever dog he is. The time involved on this first lesson varies from dog to dog, but shouldn't last longer than about fifteen minutes. When you have achieved the first objective of ten paces without pulling, give the dog a big fuss and let him off the lead for a romp. Don't overdo the practice sessions – short regular lessons are far more beneficial than one or two long ones. Puppies especially, have a relatively short attention span, and you will only bore the puppy by training for more than fifteen minutes at a time, for a maximum of three times a day. Leave at least a couple of hours between each session.

Over a few weeks of regular practice, provided you are completely consistent, don't lose your temper, reward the dog lavishly all the time he is getting it right and keep the training sessions fun, you will have a dog who, whilst not walking 'to heel', will be walking nicely without pulling, making the whole process much more enjoyable for both of you!

Head collars encourage the dog not to pull by restraining the dog's head.

If you still find you are having difficulty getting the dog to walk nicely, you could try one of the head collars which are now available for dogs. They have the effect of encouraging the dog not to pull, by restraining the dog's head. They do take some getting used to though, and not all dogs will accept them. If you elect to try one, take the dog to the pet shop with you when you go, so that you firstly get the right size, and secondly so that you can be shown how to fit the head collar and how it works.

Coming When Called

Teaching a dog to come back when you want him is one of those things that is so easy to get wrong! The problem usually occurs when you expect the dog to return whilst out on exercise, where he's having fun and freedom, before you have shown him indoors *what* is expected when you call him. If he doesn't come to you indoors, each and every time you call him, you can be sure that when he is outside, with all the interesting smells and distractions that are present, he certainly will not want to give up his liberty in a hurry!

You may also have made the problem worse by acting illogically (as far as the dog is concerned) when he does eventually decide to come back, after you have been calling him for ages. It may be that you are late for an appointment, or it is pouring with rain (or both!), and you have been standing in the park, calling and calling, whilst your dog is either playing with another dog, or investigating the bushes. Finally he comes back. You are now very cross, so of course you are not very happy with him. On goes the lead, and off you march. You know, of course, that the dog understands that you are cross, and his freedom has been ended, because he was slow in coming back! *Oh no he doesn't!* What he learns from your behaviour is that coming back to you is very unrewarding, as you are so cross when he does return to you. And not only that, his liberty is taken away! Staying away from you is therefore much more fun and rewarding, as he keeps his freedom and can do what he wants.

Another easily developed habit is only calling the dog back when it is time to go home. The dog then very quickly learns that being called signifies the end of his freedom, so he is therefore reluctant to come back.

Getting it Right

Probably the most important underlying factor is the dog's expectancy when he hears his name being used. Does he only hear his name when something is being offered, or does he hear his name several times a day when he is not expected to respond? Usually, when the dog first arrives in the house, his name is used frequently during interaction with him, so that you can teach him his name. What then tends to happen is you, and the rest of the family, start using his name conversationally, when you are not expecting him to respond, i.e. you talk about the dog to one another, perhaps telling them what the dog has been up to whilst they were out of the house. Had you been observing the dog when you first started talking about him, rather than to him, you would have noticed that when he first heard his name being used, he would probably have looked up from whatever he was doing. Then, because no clear indication was given to him to elicit a response, he would have looked away and continued with what he was doing. That is how the rot sets in! He learns to ignore his name.

Because it is human nature to want to talk *about* the dog without always wanting the dog to come to us, the easiest way around this is slightly to adapt the dog's name when you want him to come to you, and *only* use that adaptation when you are calling the dog. Coupled with the dog receiving a worthwhile reward for responding, you will condition the dog always to return when he hears the slightly varied sound, whilst you can still talk about him to one another, using the original name. As an example, let's assume you have called your dog 'Ben'. You could adapt that to 'Bennyboy' when you want him to come to you. The name 'Molly' could be adapted to 'Mollypups', 'Sacha' could be 'Sachapash', 'Cassie' could be 'Cass-Cass', and so on. One of my own favourites I used with one of my dogs, who was named 'Otto' – he became 'Spottyboy', only don't expect me to explain how that was arrived at!

Once you've selected a new calling name, then you need to show the dog what is expected when that sound is used – this is where the food comes in again, firstly with the dog's daily meals, and then with titbits.

Dogs very quickly learn their mealtime routines – they know when it is time to be fed! Before you start preparing his meal, make sure that he is out of the room, possibly being held by someone else, but ensure that he has clear access through to you. Get the food ready, then, holding it just in front of you, at waist height, call the dog with his new calling name. He will have already heard the food being prepared and he will have certainly smelt it, so as he is released from being held, once you have called him, he will probably arrive at ninety miles an hour in front of you! Reward him verbally and give him his food immediately. Repeat this same procedure before every mealtime for at least a week.

Please don't make the dog sit when he reaches you. You want him to learn that he is being rewarded with his food for coming when called and NOT for sitting. Dog logic works on a "last behaviour offered is what the reward is for" basis. If, when he reaches you after being called, you then tell him to sit, then feed him, the dog will associate the reward of his food for sitting, rather than coming when called.

After a couple of days of the mealtime rewarding, you can start with titbit training for recalls too. Start when the dog is literally next to you, say lying beside you when you're watching TV. Have the titbits handy and, when he is not looking at you, use his new recall name once, in a pleasant tone. When he looks up at you, or sits up to get even closer, reward him with a titbit, plus a verbal reward and a cuddle. You need to back up the titbit rewards with verbal and physical praise each time you use them, as eventually you will be dispensing with them most of the time. The dog needs to understand that rewards are not only of the edible variety!

Slowly build up the distance when you are recalling indoors, during that first week. Start with the dog a couple of feet away, then five, then ten feet and so on. Only instant response from the dog gets rewarded. If you have to call more than twice, do not give him the titbit when he does get to you. He has to understand that the second he hears his name, he must return to you for the food, otherwise he doesn't get it.

During all this preparation time, you must not let the dog

roam free whilst on exercise – you don't want to undo the training which you are doing indoors by putting it to the test before you are ready.

After that first week, you will then be ready to try the dog outside. There is one more part of the plot to follow though! For the past seven days, you have been conditioning the dog to return to you, on hearing his recall name, and in return being rewarded with either his meal or titbits. Once he is running free outside, there will be more distractions, which may encourage the dog to delay coming immediately, so you will need a slight edge! You're going to make sure that he will come back, by taking him out hungry!

Assuming the dog is fed twice a day, morning and evening, on the day BEFORE you are going to test out the recall whilst the dog is running free, *don't feed him the evening meal!* Make sure that he has access to water, as he can tolerate being deprived of food for a short while, but he *must* have water. You may feel very guilty, as the dog will probably start reminding you that dinner is due, but don't weaken. Think of the years ahead with a dog who is a pleasure to take out off the lead. Don't give him any titbits either. Be determined. Next day, *don't feed him his morning meal either*. Instead, prepare his morning meal in at least ten individual portions, in plastic bags. It may be a bit messy, but again, remember your long term aim and don't be put off. You've now got a very hungry dog on your hands. Take him out, with the plastic bags of food in your pockets. When you get to your usual walking place, let him off the lead, and as he starts to go away from you IMMEDIATELY call him back, take hold of his collar and give him one of the portions of food, plus a huge cuddle. Always hold the collar first before releasing the food to the dog. If you don't, he may well end up snatching the food from your hand and running off again. Holding him also gives you the opportunity to be 'in charge', by giving him his freedom again – after a few seconds, give the dog permission to 'go play' and let him go. Leave him a couple of minutes again, then repeat the procedure again. Do this throughout the walk, saving one last portion for when the walk is over and you need to re-attach him to his lead. You should now have a dog who has earned his breakfast, by coming back to you each time he was called (with his new recall name).

He can have his evening meal as usual, but all his breakfasts for at least the next week should be 'earned' whilst out walking. That should be long enough to have built up the conditioning in the dog's mind that being called means he gets fed *and* cuddled. After that first week, you can resume feeding normally at home, but save all the titbits for when you are out walking, making him earn them by coming when called.

Keep up with the praise and cuddles when he returns to you, and always use a happy sounding voice when you call him – don't ever take him for granted and NEVER lose your temper. Either of those reactions from you will result in the dog refusing to return to you, and finding other, more interesting and rewarding things to do.

Retrieving
Most dogs will quite naturally want to chase after articles thrown for them. The difficult part is getting them to return the articles, so that they can be thrown again! Of course, you should not start with retrieving until you have taught the dog to come back to you!

One word of caution here – if you want the dog to fetch a ball, please make sure that the ball is bigger than the dog's throat. As an example, a tennis ball could easily get lodged in the throat of a Labrador or German Shepherd Dog. At the risk of being a killjoy, even throwing sticks can be dangerous – if the stick does not land flat, but 'javelins" into the ground, the dog could impale himself on it. There are many purpose designed toys available from your pet shop which are safe for the dog to chase and bring back to you.

If you want your dog to play "fetch", then you have to be very careful about chastising the dog if he should run off with an inappropriate article indoors – if he should 'steal' a shoe, for example, and you shout and run after him, all he learns is that the shoe must be very important, as you are trying so hard to take it away from him. This actually encourages him to hang onto it. The shoe becomes prey in the mind of the dog, and basic instincts will come to the fore – he may even show signs of aggression if you try and take it away from him. After that, he will most certainly not want to bring back a play article in the park. Whilst you don't want to encourage the dog to steal things, what you should do when he has an inappropriate article in his mouth is to encourage him to bring it to you, and reward him with a titbit when he does. This will not stop him taking things, but it will stop him running off with them! It may also help enforce the rule which all members of the family should adhere to – don't leave things around that you wouldn't want the dog to pick up!

If you start off indoors, rewarding him with a titbit when he brings his toys to you, that behaviour will be repeated when you throw a toy for him outside.

Perhaps at some stage you may want to do more formal obedience with your dog, with a view to entering obedience competitions. A formal retrieve will be much easier to teach if you have started off as described above, having already conditioned the dog that bringing the retrieve article back is a good thing, as he gets rewarded for doing so.

Remaining in a Position
Depending on your personal requirements, you can teach the dog to "WAIT", and you can teach the dog to "STAY". Each means something different, so it is vital not to confuse the dog between the two.

"WAIT"
This command will teach the dog that it is not appropriate to move forward until he is called, for example when you want to let him out of the car. It would obviously be very unsafe to simply open the car door and allow him to jump out immediately, possibly when the car is parked on a busy road.

To begin teaching, take the dog in the car and park in a quiet spot, well away from the road. As you go to open the door, calmly give the "wait" command. If he should attempt to push through the door, gently close it again, without saying

As you go to open the door, calmly give the "wait" command.

anything and of course ensuring that you don't shut any part of him in the door! Each time you go to open the door, repeat the command "wait". Each time he attempts to push through, close the door again. Eventually, you will find that you can open the door further and further each time, until the dog waits whilst the door is opened fully. Place your hand on the dog's collar, praise him for waiting and give him a titbit. Take hold of his lead and call him forward, out of the car, using the same calling command that you will have taught him for coming when called.

You can further enforce the "wait" command at feeding times. After you have called him for his food, and rewarded him for coming with a small handful of his food, you can tell him to "sit" and "wait". Place the food bowl on the floor (or feeding stand), and repeat the wait command. If he attempts to move, quietly pick the food up again. Then repeat the procedure, until the dog does not attempt to move, at which time you can give him an appropriate command, such as "OK" or "that'll do", and allow him to have the food. The dog will quickly learn that after the "wait" command has been given he is expected to remain where he is temporarily, until he is told to come forward.

"STAY"

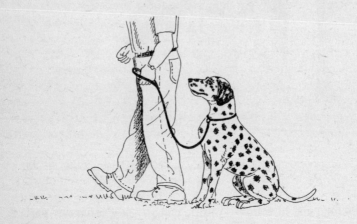

"STAY".

Unlike waiting, which is used for stopping forward movement for a few seconds before you give him another command to move towards you, "stay" is used when the dog is commanded either "sit" or "down", told to remain there whilst you move, and to stay in that position *until you return to him* and give him permission to move.

As an example, you may want the dog to accompany you to the front door when a stranger calls. You certainly will not want the dog to rush through the door, possibly getting onto the road, nor do you want him to move forward to greet the person at the door – you simply wish him to remain in one position, under control, whilst you deal with the caller.

Another good reason for teaching "stay" is in the case of domestic accidents, like broken glass on the floor. You don't want to step over the glass to remove the dog to another room, and you certainly don't want the dog walking through the glass to get to you.

Start by sitting the dog beside you, attached to his lead, as if you were about to set off walking. Make sure that you do not put any tension on the lead. Say the word "stay" calmly but firmly. If the dog is sitting on your left side, slowly move your right foot forward, as though you were going to take a step forward, then place it back by your left foot. (If the dog is sitting on your right, you would move your left foot.) You want to take two or three of these 'dummy' steps forward, calmly saying "stay", without the dog moving. By moving the foot furthest away from the dog, he is less likely to get up immediately. If he should try and move, either by lying down or moving forward, calmly put him back in the original position and start again.

When you can move your foot five times without him attempting to follow, take one step forward and turn and face him. Keep repeating the "stay" command gently, at the same time verbally rewarding him, saying "good STAY". Don't sound too excited, or he will get up, and use a gentle tone. Try and aim for about five seconds in front, and then, still saying "good STAY", step back to the side. Don't let him move immediately you return to the side, or he may start to associate your return with him getting up. Keep him staying at your side for at least three seconds, stroking him calmly on the top of his head. Then gently take a step *backwards*, at the same time telling the dog "that'll do" and turning his head slightly towards you, encouraging the dog to move backwards as you do, and releasing him from the exercise. You are aiming at conditioning the dog so that he only ever moves backwards after completing a stay, thus discouraging him from breaking the stay by moving forwards.

Don't be in too much of a hurry to let go of the lead, or get further away. Over about a week, you should aim for leaving the dog for fifteen seconds, with you standing in front, the length of the lead away, but still loosely holding onto it. Slowly, over several weeks, you can build up both the time and the distance, but you want to aim at stability before distance.

More Advanced Training

Once you have completed the basic training, and if you and your dog have enjoyed learning together, you may want to continue your dog's education, perhaps with the ultimate goal of competing in the various forms of obedience that have become popular. Any dog can be taught more advanced obedience, and even though breeds such as Border Collies, German Shepherd Dogs, Labradors and Retrievers tend to proliferate, there is no reason why your crossbreed or Terrier could not do well in competition.

Obedience Competitions

You should find a training club with instructors who specialise in motivational training techniques and who can advise you on the finer points required in the ring. Your dog should be energetic and willing to play with you to achieve the best results, and you will also need to be enthusiastic and determined. To train a dog to the high standard required demands a regular commitment of time and effort and a self-disciplined approach to your technique. The best way to find out if this is the sport for you is to attend some shows as a spectator and talk to experienced competitors – most are happy to help but try not to approach them as they are about to enter the ring!

Shows take place all over the country at various levels – Exemption, Limited, Open and Championship. Exemption shows are often held in conjunction with other events such as fêtes and may have one or two classes suitable for those new to the sport. At this level your dog does not need to be registered with the Kennel Club. If you wish to compete at Limited, Open or Championship shows, registration with the Kennel Club is compulsory. If you have a crossbreed or Mongrel, or an unregistered Border Collie, you will need to apply to the Obedience and Working Trials Register at the Kennel Club. If you have a pedigree dog, you should already have the registration certificate from the breeder and have had the ownership transferred to your name (see page 46). If you wish to enter a show before you have received your registration or transfer certificate you must add NAF (Name Applied For) or TAF (Transfer Applied For) after your dog's name on the entry form.

Exemption shows are often advertised in the local press. There is a publication called *Dog Training Weekly* which gives details of forthcoming shows, plus show reports, and also contains some interesting training articles. *DTW* is only available by postal subscription – see page 155 for details.

At all Kennel Club registered shows there are up to five classes covering different levels. Pre-Beginners is the lowest class and involves Heel work, both on and off the lead, a Recall and a Sit and Down Stay. The other classes are Beginners, Novice, Class A, Class B and Class C. Exercises in the higher classes include Scent Discrimination and Distant Control, as well as more advanced heel work and retrieving.

By winning three of the highest classes – Championship C – under three different judges, a dog can gain the title of Obedience Champion. For dogs who have won their way through the classes there is also the award known as the Obedience Warrant, signified by the letters O.W. after the dog's name. Each year at Crufts, all dogs and bitches that have won a Championship C in the previous year are invited to take part in the Kennel Club Obedience Championships. At this level competition is at an extremely high standard, with even minor faults resulting in loss of points.

Competitive obedience can be a very rewarding hobby, with the opportunity to make new friends and have fun with your dog. It is relatively inexpensive and requires no complicated equipment. You don't need an expensive dog either – many people compete successfully with rescued dogs. For the younger competitor there are also special classes arranged by the Kennel Club Junior Organisation, and for all well-trained pet dogs there is the Kennel Club Good Citizen Scheme, which is a test rather that a competition.

Working Trials
Working Trials predate Obedience Competitions and have
their roots in service dog training. They were designed as a
practical test of working ability and cover a wide range of
activities including nose work and agility.

There are five different stakes – Companion Dog (CD),
Utility Dog (UD), Working Dog (WD), Tracking Dog (TD)
and Patrol Dog (PD). Dogs which achieve a qualifying mark
in each group of exercises within a class at a Championship
Trial are entitled to have the letters CD, UD, WD, TD or PD
after their names. In addition, winners of TD or PD classes at
Championship Trials are awarded Working Trial Certificates,
which count towards the title of Working Trials Champion.
The CD and UD stakes have jumps that relate to the height of
the dog and there is consequently more variety in the breeds
that are entered. The higher stakes have full height jumps and
the most common breeds entered are German Shepherds and
Border Collies/Working Sheepdogs, with some Labradors,
Retrievers and a few other larger working breeds.

As Working Trials include nose work exercises such as
searching and tracking, they are usually held on private land
and therefore are not so accessible to spectators as some other
canine sports. To get started in trials, you will need a good
standard of obedience, a fit dog with sound hips and a love of
the outdoors! The Kennel Club can provide a list of Working
Trial Societies that will be able to help with further information and advice. Working Trials is a more specialist sport than
Competitive Obedience and you may have to travel longer
distances for tuition and competitions.

Agility
Agility competitions are one of the more recent sports to
develop, but have quickly gained a following with competitors
and spectators. It is extremely rewarding for the dogs, as it
gives them something really interesting to do and, like obedience competitions, keeps the dog's brain active in a positive
way. Like the other sports, Kennel Club registration is a must,
and dogs must be 18 months or over to compete in agility. The

main reason for this is that the dog's bones may be damaged by jumping at an early age and it is recommended that training does not start until the dog is at least one year old – later still with the larger breeds.

You will need to be physically fit, as you have to run around the ring with the dog as he goes over or through each obstacle. Obstacles range from a variety of different jumps, rather like those used in show jumping, to more specialised equipment such as weaving poles, tunnels and walkways. Accuracy is an important feature – not only must the dog jump cleanly and follow the correct course to avoid penalty points, but on some obstacles the dog must touch marked contact points. In addition, time penalties may be added to the total score if the dog fails to meet the set time for the course. A clear round is therefore quite an achievement and is often rewarded with a special rosette.

Agility competitions have become very popular and attract large entries. The standard is very high and there is sometimes very little difference in marks between the placings. There are various classes, including some for smaller dogs – known as mini-agility – and it is great fun to see these little dogs racing around the course at top speed. Dogs taking part in agility do enjoy themselves and can get over-excited so it is important that basic obedience control is attained before tackling agility.

Agility training often takes place at indoor riding schools where the facilities are suitable for jumping, and there are classes held all over the country. As with the other sports, the Kennel Club can provide details of clubs registered with them.

Showing
Unlike obedience, agility or working trials, showing classes are judged on the look and conformation of your dog, and on how he or she matches up to the breed standard, as laid down by the Kennel Club. It helps if you mention to the breeder, when buying, that you would like to show your puppy, so that you purchase a good quality puppy initially.

As well as being obedient in the show ring, you will need to know how to show your particular breed, so attending a

Ringcraft Training Club is very helpful. You will encounter some of the atmosphere and distractions that your puppy will have to cope with at shows, and at the same time will also receive advice on standing and handling your puppy from knowledgeable enthusiasts. Joining fees are not high, and most good clubs run regular match nights, which provide good experience for you and your puppy, emulating where possible what will happen in the show ring. Your puppy must be at least six months old before you can enter him in a show, and must be registered with the Kennel Club, with the exception of Exemption shows (see page 88), which are a really good place to start your showing career. You can enter these types of show on the actual show day. The other types of shows are as follows:

1. Limited Shows – These are limited to members of the club which is running them, so you have to join that particular club in order to compete. The membership fee is usually small, and you can usually join the club when you receive your entry form. These shows are advertised in the dog press, and entry is always in advance – you cannot enter on the day of the show.

2. Open Shows – These are held throughout the country and will have individual classes for most breeds. If your particular breed does not have an individual class, you can enter in what is called Any Variety – where you will be competing against different breeds. You do not need to be a member of the organising club to compete at these shows. Again, they are advertised in the dog press, and you must enter your dog in advance of the actual show.

3. Championship Shows – This is where you will meet stiff competition, with classes being quite large. Entry into a Championship show is the same as that for Open shows. A dog can only become a show champion by competing and winning at a Championship show. The classes for your breed will be split into separate classes for dogs and bitches. When all classes for dogs (males) have been judged, all class winners then compete against each other

for the title of Best Dog, and this dog will be awarded a Challenge Certificate. The Reserve dog (2nd) will be awarded the Reserve Challenge Certificate. The bitches are then judged, for Best Bitch and Reserve Bitch, and again they will receive a Challenge Certificate and Reserve Challenge Certificate. The Best Dog and Best Bitch then compete against each other for the title of Best of Breed. The winner will then go forward into what is called the Group judging, where all other winning dogs from breeds in the same group definition compete for the title Best of Group. When all Group winners are decided, they then compete against each other for the title Best in Show. A dog or bitch must win three separate challenge certificates, under three different judges, to become a champion. The last of the three certificates must be won when the dog is over one year old.

4.   Crufts – Dogs who win at Championship Shows, or who gain Best Puppy in Show, Best in Show and Reserve Best in Show at an all breeds open show, can qualify to compete at Crufts, Only a dog of nine months or over can compete – if a dog has qualified but will be too young to compete, he or she will be able to compete the following year without further qualification.

Showing your dog can be great fun, and you will meet other like-minded people and owners of the same breed as your dog. Do remember though, that your dog is first and foremost a pet, and not an ornament, and remember too, if you show your dog, that whatever the outcome you always go home with the best dog!

Information about all these types of training can often be obtained from your local library or veterinary surgery, or by contacting The Kennel Club (see Appendix, page 155).

8

NEUTERING AND BREEDING

If you are not going to breed from your dog, it is generally better from both a behavioural and medical point of view to have him or her neutered.

Bitches – Spaying

A female dog will come into season usually every six months, starting at any time from six months of age, depending on breed and size. The season will last approximately three weeks, during which time she must be kept completely away from all male dogs. Some bitches will actively attempt to find a mate, so great care has to be taken to make sure she does not escape from the house or garden whilst she is in season.

Many bitches have what is known as a phantom pregnancy, where her head will tell her she is pregnant, even if she has not been anywhere near a male dog! She may show physical signs of pregnancy, such as producing milk and 'mothering' toys. She may undergo changes in temperament too, perhaps becoming snappy or possessive.

Physically, an unspayed bitch could be more prone to mammary tumours (like breast cancer in women) than an unspayed bitch and older unspayed bitches are at risk of their womb becoming diseased, resulting in a possibly life threatening condition called Pyometra (see Chapter 9, page 106).

Spaying will prevent any risk of pregnancy and stop her seasons. The operation involves a general anaesthetic and removal of the ovaries and womb. The bitch will have stitches, which will be removed by your vet, usually after ten days. Until the stitches are removed, her exercise should be limited to gentle walks on the lead. Once the stitches are removed, she can return to normal exercise. You will need to watch her weight after she is spayed, as it can cause a slight metabolic change, which could lead to weight gain. Take advice from your vet to prevent this happening.

The best time to have your bitch spayed is after she has had her first season. Coming into season signifies that the bitch has matured, both mentally and physically. Although it is quite common nowadays to have bitches spayed before they have had a season, it can occasionally have a detrimental effect on the bitch from a psychological point of view – without going through the natural process of maturing and having that first season, some bitches can become mentally agitated when their season would normally have been due.

If the worst happens and your unspayed bitch does accidentally get mated, she can have what is call a misalliance injection. The injection is given on the third and fifth day after the mating, and will usually prevent her from having puppies on that occasion, although there is a small risk that the pregnancy will continue.

Males – Castration
The majority of male dogs are much easier to live with if they are castrated. They tend not to be aggressive to other males, and generally are more loving and compliant with their human family. There *are* people who assume that it will solve every training problem, which it won't – there is no replacement for basic training. It won't necessarily stop problems like territory marking, or indeed his knowing the difference between a dog or a bitch!

The operation stops the production of testosterone, the male hormone which tends to be at the root of aggression. It *does not* turn your male dog into a pathetic, weak animal, as some people believe, and as previously mentioned, only changes his temperament *for the better*.

Although not such a big procedure as spaying, it is still done under a general anaesthetic. The dog will have stitches at the site from where the testicles have been removed, and you must ensure that the dog does not lick or bite the stitches. He will need restricted gentle exercise on the lead for a few days, or possibly until the stitches are removed by your vet, usually ten to fourteen days later. The dog will probably recover from the effects of the anaesthetic within twenty-four to forty-eight hours after the operation, and you will probably be surprised at how quickly the dog recovers generally – unlike humans, dogs do not feel sorry for themselves after surgery or injury, and seem to accept the situation remarkably quickly.

Again, as with bitches, you can have a male dog neutered when he is still a puppy, but my advice would be that, unless your dog has severe, sexually-based behavioural problems, it is best to wait until he is at least nine months old. It is my experience that, at whatever age the dog is when he is castrated, the mental maturing process tends to stop once the castration is done. You could therefore have a puppy castrated at four months old, and when he is, for example, two years old, he could still have the mental age of a four month old puppy!

Breeding

Breeding from a bitch, or using a male as a stud dog, should really be left to the knowledgeable expert. However, if you are thinking seriously about using your dog to breed from, you should at least have some idea of what you could be letting yourself in for.

Stud Dogs

If you own a male dog, you may feel that as you won't be the one responsible for looking after any puppies, that it is an easy way of making money, i.e. from stud fees.

What you should be aware of is how, once your dog has been used, his temperament may be changed forever. He may continually seek out other bitches whilst on exercise, refusing to return when called – the reproductive instinct is stronger than any other! He may well become aggressive with other male dogs, seeing them as a challenge to his supremacy. He may start mounting members of his human family, particularly the children.

If you are prepared for these possible changes in temperament, and decide to go ahead, you must first ensure that your dog is healthy, and does not have any genetic defects which he could pass on to his offspring. You should also have him tested to ensure that he does not carry any sexually transmitted disease, which could be passed on to the bitch during mating. Even if the dog has not been used for stud before, he could still be carrying infection, which could affect both the conception of, and viability of, any subsequent puppies. Temperamentally, he should be neither aggressive nor shy, as both these traits could be passed on to the puppies. As the stud dog owner, you must be prepared to 'entertain' the bitch and her owner in your home, when the time for mating arrives. This may last for several hours and usually requires two visits, so that the bitch can be mated twice. If you have children in the house, they should be kept well away in case of any aggression – quite often the bitch will be snappy to begin with, and you certainly would not want to risk the children getting bitten.

Having already mentioned stud fees, it may well turn out that even after two visits from the bitch, she does not get pregnant, and therefore you will not receive a stud fee.

Overall, stud dog ownership is not as simple as it first appears. It really is best to leave it to the experts – and after all, there are already thousands of unwanted dogs in this country, which you could be adding to if you allow your dog to be used.

Bitches

Even in this supposedly enlightened age, there is still the widely held myth that it is good for a bitch to have at least one litter of puppies. There is no scientific or medical evidence to back this up, whereas there have been many cases of bitches suffering medical problems, either during the birth of the puppies, or shortly afterwards.

Although it could be said that giving birth is a natural process, humans have interfered so much in the dog world that there are some breeds that have been altered by selective breeding to the extent that they cannot give birth naturally. One instance of this is with the Bulldog – the head of the Bulldog has been developed to be so large that the puppies' heads are too big to pass naturally through the birth canal and therefore have to be born by caesarean section.

In a worse case scenario, you may lose both bitch and puppies due to birthing complications, and, apart from the distress this would cause, it would also involve huge veterinary bills.

If you are determined to breed from your bitch, you should first wait until she is at least two years old, and then have her checked for any genetic defects which she could pass on to her puppies. You should also have had her tested to ensure that she is not carrying any sexually transmitted disease or infection which she may pass on to the stud dog during mating – indeed many owners of stud dogs will insist upon this. A maiden bitch could still carry infection, such as Beta Haemolytic Strep or Pasteurella, which could be passed on to the stud dog during mating. You should only breed from her if her temperament is sound. As she is the one who rears the puppies, any character defects may be passed on to her puppies, as they will learn from her example. You will also need to choose the stud dog carefully, making sure that he too has been checked for any defects, and also that he is sound in temperament. She will need to be treated for worms before she is mated, to minimise the quantity of worms which she will pass on to her unborn puppies.

Assuming your bitch becomes pregnant, you will need to ensure that she is fed the correct amounts as her pregnancy proceeds. Towards the end of the pregnancy, she may be eating more than twice her normal quantity of food. She will still need gentle exercise on the lead, to keep her body fit and supple, but you will also need to keep her away from any possible infection, to protect her and her unborn puppies.

You must have the room, time and money to be able to

house and rear the puppies properly. You are also responsible for finding good homes for all of them, and providing back-up help for the new owners. Initially, the bitch will keep her puppies and the whelping area clean, but, once the puppies start to be weaned, they will pass copious amounts of urine and faeces and it can be a very dirty business which needs clearing up frequently! Weaning a litter on to solid food is also a very time consuming, messy and expensive affair.

The puppies will need worming before they go to their new homes, and responsible breeders will provide veterinary insurance for the puppies for at least the first 4–6 weeks after they have gone to their new home. You should also provide the new owners with a copy of the pedigree certificate (where appropriate), a registration and transfer of ownership document (again if appropriate) and written details of the diet and care that the new puppy will need.

You may get extremely attached to the puppies, and will find it very upsetting when they go to their new homes. You also have to be prepared to take back any puppies if the new owners decide they cannot cope with or care for them.

Hopefully you will decide that dog breeding should be left to the experts who have the expertise and facilities to do the job properly.

9

KEEPING YOUR DOG HEALTHY

With a little common sense and luck, hopefully your dog will live a long and healthy life. There are several precautions you can take to help keep your dog fit and healthy, and to reduce the risk of your dog passing on disease to other animals.

General care

Inoculations
As a puppy, your dog will have been inoculated against distemper, hepatitis, leptospirosis, parvo virus and para influenza. You may also have had him protected against kennel cough. Regular yearly booster inoculations are vital to continue the protection (the kennel cough vaccination is done twice yearly).

Worming
Your dog should be treated for the prevention of worms at least twice a year – more often if your dog is a scavenger. There are two main groups of worms which affect dogs – roundworms and tapeworms. Worm infestation can cause abnormal hunger, diarrhoea, poor growth, itching around the bottom and general loss of condition.

Untreated dogs can pass worms on to other dogs, via the eggs which are deposited in the faeces when the dog goes to the toilet. The eggs are then moved around by the wind and on the soles of people's shoes, or by sticking to the feet of passing dogs. That dog then licks himself and ingests the eggs, causing the dog to becoming infested.

An unwormed dog could also cause a disease in humans called Visceral Larva Migrans, which is caused by ingesting the egg of the roundworm Toxocara Canis. Children are particularly at risk, as they tend to put their hands near or into their mouths, especially if they should do so after touching a piece of ground infected with the worm eggs, or if they are petting a dog who has worms. The egg can enter via contact from hand to mouth, and, in very severe cases, can cause blindness or mental retardation. Although these cases are rare, simple precautions such as always washing your hands after handling a dog, particularly a strange dog, and ensuring that your dog is regularly treated for worms, will prevent this from happening. It is worth noting that unwormed cats carry a similar worm – Toxocara Cati – which can also cause the same disease in humans as Toxocara Canis.

You must treat your dog for worms, even if you never see any actual evidence – the eggs which pass from the dog via the faeces are minute. If you should see what appear to be small grains of rice in the faeces and around the anal area, that is very clear evidence that your dog has a severe infestation of tapeworms. If you see what look like strands of spaghetti in the faeces or vomit, you can be sure that your dog has a roundworm infestation.

Fleas

All dogs are extremely susceptible to fleas (as indeed are cats). Only fastidious attention to flea control will ensure that your dog is kept clear of these prolific parasites. There are many different types of flea prevention products available from your vet, and he or she can advise you on the most suitable for your particular needs. Fleas are around for the entire year – not just the summer, as some people think. The larvae can remain dormant in your home for many months, and will hatch out when conditions are appropriate, then jump onto your dog for a meal. They do not live on the dog, but simply use him as a source of food. They will live in your home, and anywhere where the dog regularly goes, such as the car. You must treat the home and car regularly too, to kill off the larvae and any adult fleas. They especially like warm areas, such as the carpet beneath the radiators, the settee, or the bedroom! One of the best ways to prevent fleas getting a hold in your home is regular use of the vacuum cleaner. This will suck up the eggs around the edges of the carpets, before they have a chance to hatch. As the flea is also the intermediate host of the tape-worm, you can see that flea control is doubly important.

Ticks
Although not as common as the flea, dogs can get ticks even if they live in the town. Hedgehogs carry these parasites, as well as farm animals. Adult ticks live on the host, sucking the blood, then fall off and lay their eggs. The eggs attach themselves to grasses and branches, and wait for the next host to pass by, when they attach themselves, and the cycle starts again. You may well not notice the tick to begin with, and it is only when the tick begins to grow that you will see a wart-like swelling on the dog, which can grow up to 1cm as it engorges with blood. Ticks are usually found on the legs, chest, neck or face. DON'T be tempted to pull it off – if you do, you will probably leave the mouth parts behind, which may become infected and cause an abscess. Your vet can remove the whole tick safely. Ticks can also transmit disease to humans.

Lice
Less common than either the flea or tick, lice can infest the run down or stray dog. There are two types – those which bite and feed off dead skin, and sucking lice which feed from the blood of the dog. Flea prevention products (available from your veterinary surgeon) should also prevent this unpleasant para-site from invading your dog.

Grooming the Dog
Regular brushing and combing will not only keep your dog tangle free, but will also help you spot any sign of the previously mentioned parasites. At the same time as grooming the dog, you can also inspect and examine him for any cuts, bumps or sores (as described in Chapter 6, page 61).

Common Ailments and Infectious Diseases

The following section deals with the more common illnesses and afflictions which you may encounter with your dog. It is NOT intended to be a self-help guide to treating your dog. *Always seek veterinary advice whenever your dog is showing signs of illness or discomfort.*

Anal Glands

The anal glands are two small scent glands, one on either side of the anus, just underneath the tail. The glands contain a very strong smelling substance, which the dog can expel after defecation, either to mark his territory, or when he is feeling very fearful. Some dogs can have problems with these glands, and they may need emptying from time to time – a procedure which is definitely one to leave for your vet to perform. Occasionally abscesses may form in the glands, or they can become impacted. You may notice the dog appearing to 'slide' along on his bottom, as he attempts to relieve the irritation of the impacted glands. If the dog continues to have problems with these glands, they can be surgically removed.

Cystitis

This is an infection in the bladder and causes the dog to pass frequent small amounts of urine, which may contain specks of blood. It is more common in bitches, but can affect males too. Treatment with antibiotics is required, and if you suspect that your dog may have cystitis, try to take a fresh sample of the dog's urine with you when you take him or her to the vet. By testing the urine, the vet will be able to make a positive diagnosis, and treatment can start immediately.

Care should be taken to prevent urine scald around the urinary opening. Bathing the area with warm water, careful drying and then applying calendula powder will help both prevent and relieve the scalding.

Diarrhoea

An upset tummy can be an indication of many conditions, including worms, bacterial infection, viruses, allergic reaction to food, or poisoning. Withhold all food immediately, ensure the dog has access to water. It may be simply a 'one off' caused perhaps by something the dog has eaten which disagrees with him. Provided there is no blood in the diarrhoea, and the dog is showing no other signs of illness, starving him for 24 hours should sort his tummy out. If he is still passing runny motions after 24 hours, seek veterinary advice. Once diagnosis and treatment are complete, it is often helpful to give your dog a daily spoonful of plain, live yoghurt – this will help replenish the friendly natural gut bacteria. Feed a light diet for a few days, such as cooked chicken and rice, or cooked fish and rice.

Ear Infections
Signs of ear problems can range from increased warmth of the ear on touching, sensitivity of the area, drooping ears, holding the head to one side, scratching at the ears, a discharge from the ear, or continual shaking of the head. This could be due to ear mites, an ear infection, a trapped grass seed, or a foreign body stuck in the ear. *Do not attempt to treat by poking anything in the ear or administering any liquid into the ear.* You could permanently damage the ear and the hearing. Consult your vet for diagnosis and treatment.

Eclampsia
This condition affects bitches who have just had puppies, either soon after the birth or during the nursing stages, but occasionally it may happen just before the bitch whelps. It is caused by a reduced level of calcium in the blood, normally due to the demands of the nursing puppies on the bitch, which depletes her supply. Signs could be some or all of the following: loss of appetite, high fever, possibly convulsions, restlessness, panting, nervousness, stiffness, muscular spasms or twitching. Immediate veterinary treatment is essential, as this condition is life-threatening.

Eyes
One of the more common ailments which can affect the dog's eyes is conjunctivitis. It is typified by a pale greeny-white

discharge at the inner corner of one or both eyes, and the eyes may look sore and red. Early treatment from your vet, either with an antibiotic cream or drops, will quickly clear up this condition.

More serious eye conditions, such as Cataracts or Entropion, usually need surgery to rectify them. Cataracts can affect dogs in the same way as they can affect people, and are more commonly seen in the older dog. The lens has a cloudy appearance, and the dog will possibly be showing signs of not seeing clearly. Entropion is a condition where the eyelid turns inwards and, as a result, the eyelashes then come into contact with the surface of the eye, rubbing against the eye and causing ulceration. This condition is often inherited, and there is a screening system available, where owners can have future breeding stock checked to see if they carry this condition. Occasionally, Entropion can develop after frequent bouts of conjunctivitis, especially if the conjunctivitis remains untreated for long periods.

Heatstroke

A dog's normal body temperature is higher than ours – between 38.3 and 38.7° centigrade – and as such they feel the heat more than we do. Add to that the addition of a thick fur coat and the very limited ability to dissipate heat – by panting and through the pads under their feet – and you can see how dogs will suffer in hot weather. It is a wise precaution not to exercise your dog during the heat of the day, and not to allow over-exertion. If your dog is unfortunate enough to suffer from heatstroke, there are some immediate first-aid procedures you can perform. Signs of heatstroke are panting, profuse salivation, vomiting and general weakness. Remove the dog to an area of shade, preferably where there is a breeze, and apply ice packs and/or cold water to the head, neck and shoulder area. If the dog is able to drink, offer him *small* quantities of water at regular intervals. Continue the treatment and seek veterinary help immediately. Whilst on the subject of heatstroke, NEVER leave your dog in the car when the sun is shining. Every year, there are reports of dogs dying in cars – the owner may only have left them for a few minutes, but even with the windows open, cars can become ovens in minutes. It is not just the heat that kills, but also the lack of air circulation – **don't take the risk!**

Kennel Cough
Despite implication from the name, kennel cough can be contracted anywhere, not just in kennels. It is a condition caused by one or more of several agents – bacteria, virus and mycoplasma – spread by droplet, and extremely contagious. The cough is usually harsh, as if something is stuck in the throat. Sometimes there is also a clear, watery discharge from the eyes and nose, and the dog may appear to be a little fussy over food. Veterinary advice should be taken, as antibiotics may be needed to prevent secondary infection in the chest. A teaspoonful of clear honey given at regular intervals will help soothe the throat, as will a spoonful of low fat vanilla ice cream. Your dog will need to be kept away from other dogs all the time he is still coughing, and for two weeks following cessation of coughing, as he could still be infectious. Your vet can advise you about vaccinating your dog against kennel cough.

Pyometra
This is a condition which only affects unspayed bitches and is an infection of the uterus. It is a condition which requires urgent veterinary attention and, if left untreated, the bitch will probably die. More commonly it occurs soon after the bitch has been in season. The onset can be quite sudden – vomiting, diarrhoea, discoloured vaginal discharge, loss of appetite and excessive thirst and urination – some or all of these symptoms may be present. Occasionally a bitch will have a Closed Pyometra, where the infection remains enclosed in the uterus, and therefore there is no external evidence of a discharge. Sometimes the bitch will display similar symptoms as described above, but also may just appear to be generally lethargic, off her food and with a raised temperature. Urgent treatment is still needed. In both cases, immediate removal of the womb is the only treatment.

Skin Conditions
There is a veritable myriad of skin conditions, ranging from flea allergies, food allergies, contact allergies, mange, ring-

worm, eczema and so on. They can manifest themselves in a variety of ways: dry skin, flaky skin, redness, itching, greasy hair, pimples, scabs, hair loss, foul smelling skin. Indeed, canine skin problems are now one of the biggest reasons why dogs visit the vet. All skin conditions need prompt attention, so don't leave it in the hope that it will clear itself up – it won't! It is important to know that two of these skin conditions are transmittable to humans.

Mange

Demodectic Mange is caused by a microscopic mite that lives in the hair follicles. This cannot be passed on to humans, but Sarcoptic Mange, which is caused by a mite which burrows into the skin, *is* contagious to humans.

Ringworm

Ringworm is caused by a fungus, not a worm. It grows on the skin, starting at a centre point and growing outwards in a ring shape. As it grows, the hair and skin become thickened and irritated, and the hair sometimes breaks. Ringworm is contagious to humans.

Snake Bites

In the British Isles we are fortunate that there is only one poisonous snake – the adder. This is a protected species, and generally causes humans little or no problem, as the adder prefers to keep out of our way. In warm weather the adder likes to come above ground to bask in the sunshine. Usually, the vibrations caused by our footsteps warn the adder of our approach and they will quickly disappear. Unfortunately dogs, being lighter and more inquisitive of areas off the beaten track do occasionally get bitten, usually on the foot, lower leg, chest, neck or nose. You may not be immediately aware if your dog does get bitten. Sometimes they may yelp, but it could be that the first sign is either a swelling where the dog has been bitten, or you may indeed not notice anything until the dog collapses. If you can avoid making the dog walk, so much the better – any exertion will accelerate the blood circulation, which in turn will quicken the spread of the venom through the dog's system. If you can't carry the dog, walk him calmly to the car, keeping calm yourself so as not to cause the dog any more distress. Seek veterinary assistance immediately.

Stings

Bee and wasp stings can cause the same reaction in dogs as they do in humans. More often it is young puppies who are fascinated by the movement and buzzing sound and either try to sniff at them or catch them in their mouths. Either action can result in the puppy being stung. If stung in the mouth, head or neck area, seek veterinary assistance as the area will swell and could compromise the dog's breathing. If the dog is stung on the foot, perhaps by treading on the wasp or bee, and provided that the dog shows no sign of allergic reaction (such as distress and collapse), you should be able to treat the sting yourself. Bathe the area with vinegar for a wasp sting or with bicarbonate of soda for a bee sting. If in any doubt, contact your vet.

Teeth

A dog has 42 teeth when fully grown – 12 incisors, 4 canines, 16 premolars, 4 upper molars and 6 lower molars. Puppies have usually lost all their milk teeth by around six months old. Occasionally a milk tooth may be retained, even though the adult tooth has grown alongside. This can sometimes cause the puppy to continue destructive chewing, as he did when the adult teeth started coming through. The retained milk tooth (or teeth) will probably need to be removed, by your vet.

A dog's teeth should be cleaned regularly, to prevent decay and gum disease. A good diet, with suitable food to crunch on, plus good quality hard toys, will all help to keep tartar at bay. Canine toothpaste and brushes can be obtained from your vet and if you start cleaning the teeth from puppyhood, your dog will accept that this is part of his regular grooming routine. Start by putting a small spot of toothpaste on your finger and gently rub your finger over the dog's teeth. After doing this a few times, you can progress to using the brush. Although time-consuming, if you can clean the dog's teeth at least two or three times a week, you may well prevent expensive dental treatment in the future and save your dog from the discomfort of gingivitis (inflamed gums) or tooth decay.

Dental problems may be slow to detect. You may notice the dog choosing not to eat hard food, having unpleasant smelling breath, or salivating more than usual. Left for too long, the dog will start to lose weight. Early detection of gum or teeth disorders may save your dog from permanently losing some teeth, so regular inspection of the dog's mouth and teeth is strongly advised.

Torsion – Acute Gastric Dilation

This is an extremely serious condition, which, if left undetected or untreated, can result in death within a few hours of onset. It tends to be a condition more commonly associated with the larger, deeper chested breeds, and can occur shortly after the dog has eaten, due to excess gas production or gas which is unable to escape. This causes distension of the stomach, which in turn causes impaired blood flow. The dog will show signs of distress, salivate profusely, show an enlarged abdomen and attempt to vomit. Left untreated the dog will go into shock, and ultimately collapse and die. URGENT veterinary help is required. A further complication is when the stomach then rotates and twists (torsion), which usually requires emergency surgery.

Although the cause of gastric dilation is not completely understood, there are one or two things you can do to help prevent it reoccurring. To reduce the amount of air intake when your dog is feeding, place the bowl in a feeding stand, approximately at shoulder height to the dog. Instead of feeding the dog twice a day, feed three or four smaller meals. Restrict the amount of water the dog takes in at any one time – obviously the dog needs to drink, but don't allow him copious amounts all in one go.

Vomiting

If a dog is being sick repeatedly, it could well be just one symptom of any number of different illnesses. It may be something as simple as an upset stomach, or it could be an indication of much more serious problems, such as poisoning, kidney problems or an allergic reaction to drug treatment. If the dog is sick just once, and appears to be perfectly well in every other way, it may simply be something that he has scavenged which has caused him to vomit. Often, dogs will deliberately cause themselves to vomit, usually by first eating grass (a natural emetic), which will prompt the elimination of bile.

Obviously, if the dog is being sick, plus showing other signs of being unwell, a trip to the vet is needed.

The above are just a few of the illnesses and conditions which you may encounter at some time throughout your dog's lifetime. With common sense and by taking the right precautions, plus guidance from your veterinary surgeon, you should be able to reduce substantially any risk to your dog from illness or disease.

Although any ailment or illness should always be checked out with your vet, it is a good idea to have a simple canine first-aid kit, for use in the case of minor ailments. **Check with your vet first, before treating any condition yourself**. As a suggestion, the kit should comprise bandages, veterinary wound powder (an antiseptic powder for cuts or bites) and liquid paraffin (for aiding the digestive system if your dog is constipated).

Homeopathic and Bach Flower Remedies

Many dog owners and some vets now use a variety of alternative therapies for treating some medical conditions which haven't responded well to conventional medicine. Homeopathic and Bach Flower remedies are just two of the alternatives which may be tried at home, particularly for minor ailments. You could add the following to your first-aid kit: arnica (a homeopathic remedy for sore joints or as an aid to post-operative healing), rescue remedy (a Bach Flower remedy for the treatment of stress or nerves), calendula powder and cream (a very useful soothing remedy for stings, bites, sores and so), and finally a homeopathic snake bite remedy, available from homeopathic pharmacies, for the immediate treatment of adder bites.

Always take veterinary advice before you treat the dog yourself.

10

THE LAW AND YOUR DOG

Identification
It is a legal requirement that your dog wear a collar carrying a visible means of identifying you as his owner. Even if your dog is micro-chipped or tattooed, he must still wear this identification.

Dogs on Leads
When walking along any road, your dog must be held on a lead. No matter how well-trained your dog becomes, he can still be spooked by a loud noise or unfamiliar object, and if you are foolish enough to allow him to be walking free, he could well end up darting into the road, perhaps causing a serious accident in the process. As the person in charge of the dog, you will be held liable for any such accident, and you may well end up responsible for repairs to cars and/or property – and possible personal injury claims too.

Children Exercising Dogs
Although not yet enforceable by law, it is very irresponsible to allow unsupervised children to take a dog out. Dogs are unpredictable – all manner of things can change your placid pooch into an angry, aggressive or defensive dog. A child does not have the ability or knowledge to cope with that type of occurrence. Children are not only unpredictable themselves sometimes, but are also not physically strong enough to hold a

dog if he decides to "take off". This doesn't just apply to the larger breeds either – often the smaller dogs are more highly strung and just as likely to be frightened or goaded into unusual behaviour.

Picking Up After Your Dog

Nearly all public parks and outside recreational spaces are now designated as "pick-up" areas, as well as all pavements and grass verges. You should always carry either a plastic bag or poop-scoop and, once collected, the waste matter should either be deposited in one of the specified dog waste bins, or if not available, the waste should be taken home and disposed of hygienically. Failure to clean up after your dog could make you liable to a fine of anything up to £1000.

The Dangerous Dogs Act

This Act does not just apply to Pit Bull Terriers, or large breeds such as German Shepherd Dogs or Rottweilers. It applies to ALL dogs. Furthermore, your dog need not necessarily have bitten someone for you to be summonsed under the Act. As a dog owner, you are responsible for your dog's actions and, more importantly, how those actions are perceived by other people. *You* may know that your big friendly Labrador is only charging across the park to say "hello" to the person on the other side. That person, however, who may not even have a dog with them, sees a dog hurtling towards them and may well be very fearful, scared that your dog is going to attack them. They could see the dog as being out of control and you could be prosecuted as a result. Worse still, if they are so scared that they start to shout, or run away, that may well prompt your dog to jump at them, or to cause the dog to act out of character.

It is up to you to ensure that your dog never causes a nuisance to others, however well intentioned the dog's actions may be. The Act can be enforced against any breed of dog which is deemed to be dangerously out of control in a public place. Even if the dog has not injured anyone, if there are grounds to believe that he *may* do so, all or any of the following restrictions may be enforced:

- The dog may be destroyed.
- The owner is liable for a fine, a term of imprisonment, or both.
- The owner may be disqualified from keeping a dog, for such a period as the court deems fit.

You can see therefore how important it is that your dog is properly trained and controlled at all times.

Quarantine

After many years of discussion, the rules on quarantine have been partially changed. Quarantine has not been abolished altogether, and dogs entering the UK from most countries still have to spend six months in quarantine kennels.

Pet Passports

A new pilot Pet Travel Scheme (PETS), also known as Passport for Pets, has been introduced. Under the scheme, pet dogs and cats **resident in the UK** may visit the countries listed below and return without the need for quarantine. Dogs and cats travelling under the scheme that **come** from the following countries, and have been resident there at least for six months, may enter the UK without going into quarantine, provided they have shown a negative blood test for Rabies at least six months before they travel. The countries are: Andorra, Austria, Belgium, Denmark, Finland, France, Germany, Gibraltar, Greece, Iceland, Italy, Liechtenstein, Luxembourg, Monaco, Netherlands, Norway, Portugal, San Marino, Spain, Sweden, Switzerland, Vatican. Within some of these countries, there are certain areas which are excluded, so it is advisable to check with the Ministry of Agriculture, Fisheries & Food (MAFF), before embarking on any travel plans. Only certain air and sea routes into and out of the UK are operating under the PETS scheme, so you will need to check this with your travel operator.

Under the PETS scheme, dogs and cats from the Channel Islands, the Isle of Man and the Republic of Ireland can go to any qualifying country and return to the UK, provided they have the official certification. Jersey, Guernsey, the Isle of Man and the Republic of Ireland have each produced their own official PETS certificate.

The criteria for travelling to the countries listed above **from** the UK is as follows:

1. The dog must be fitted with a permanent number micro-chip – your own vet can do this.
2. The dog must have been vaccinated against rabies, using an approved vaccine – your own vet can do this at the time of micro-chipping. (The dog must also have booster vaccinations at required intervals.) Dogs under three months old cannot be vaccinated.
3. Thirty days after vaccination, the dog must have a blood test to check that the required antibody levels have been achieved. The blood has to be tested by a laboratory approved by MAFF. If the required levels are not achieved, the dog must be re-vaccinated and the blood tested after another thirty days.
4. The dog must have a health certificate certifying that the above criteria has been met. This certificate must be signed by an approved Local Veterinary Inspector.
5. The dog must have been treated for certain parasites and ticks 24 to 48 hours before the dog enters the UK. The dog must also have a certificate from an official vet stating that these treatments have been given. (You will need to find a vet in the country you are visiting who has the right medication and documentation.)

Although not part of the conditions, it would also be advisable to keep to your regular flea prevention routine and ensure your dog has been treated with an appropriate flea/tick product *before* leaving this country – this will then protect your dog from ticks whilst you are abroad. Only treating the dog before your return to this country will not cover the dog during your stay abroad, where he is open to infestation from ticks not found in the UK, and he could be gestating tick bite fever, without showing any signs, before the required check by a vet

24 to 48 hours before you return home. Tick bites can cause a disease called Babesia Canis, which can prove fatal, and ticks can transmit potentially serious diseases to both pets and humans, such as Babesiosis and Ehrlichiosis. Make sure the dog is protected BEFORE you travel. It would also be advisable to check with your vet about specified diseases which may be prevalent in the country you are planning to visit, but which do not occur in the UK. Your dog will not have built up any immunity to such diseases, and your vet may be able to provide preventative treatment.

Failure to adhere to any of these conditions may render the Pet Passport invalid and the dog would have to go into quarantine for six months. Any vet can micro-chip, vaccinate and take blood for testing, but only approved laboratories can carry out the blood test, and only Local Veterinary Inspectors are able to issue pet health certificates.

For dogs leaving the UK, owners should also check to see if they need a separate health certificate to show that the dog meets the health requirements of the country they are visiting. The PETS scheme is continually under review and it would be advisable to check with MAFF and/or your vet for any changes which may have been implemented since the writing of this book.

11

CARING FOR THE AGEING DOG

Not unlike humans, as a dog ages his requirements for sleep, food and exercise will change. He may develop some hearing loss, or his eyesight may deteriorate. His joints may start to stiffen and his appetite may become a little delicate. Depending on the size and breed of your dog, changes due to ageing can start any time from as early as 5 years old. Continued exercise is important, but should be adapted to his ability. Take advice from your veterinary surgeon about altering the dog's food. You may well need to change his diet, either to a proprietary 'senior' dog food, or perhaps pandering to him a little and giving him cooked chicken or fish.

As the dog ages, he must be allowed to spend more time resting, and should be protected from unwanted attention from either children or other pets. He may become a little irritable as he gets older, and will not show the same patience with youngsters as he did in his youth. He may start to dislike being left alone, so perhaps employing a dog-sitter should be considered. As time goes on, he may not be able to control his bladder or bowels quite so well, so will need more frequent trips to the garden, and may have the odd accident indoors.

Frequently, as the dog ages, people think about getting another puppy, perhaps to give the older dog a 'new lease of life'. In my experience, I have always found this to be very beneficial for both older dog and puppy alike, as the older dog tends to start to play again, with the puppy, and the pup can sometimes learn from the older, wiser dog. Of course, you must make sure that the puppy does not worry the older dog, and the pup must be trained to leave the older dog alone when he needs to rest. You must also consider how the younger dog will react, once the older dog eventually comes to the end of his life – perhaps you should think about getting another companion fairly soon, so that the younger dog is not lonely?

When To Say Goodbye
During the course of writing this book, I had to make the awful decision to have a beloved dog put to sleep, to save her any further suffering. It is something I have had to face many times during my dog-owning years, and it never gets any easier. It is also something that perhaps you don't want to think about, just as you are embarking upon your first experience of owning a dog. It is, however, an inevitable fact of life that, unless your dog dies naturally, at some stage you, as a caring, responsible owner, are going to have to make the decision to end the dog's life.

There is an expression that many dog owners use when deciding when the time should come. It is "Quality of Life" – and here I am talking about the dog's life, not the human's. In other words, is the dog still enjoying the important things in life – walking, eating and being cuddled – without pain or embarrassment at being unable to do the things he once could? It may sound strange to imply that a dog can feel embarrassment, but I know that dogs do feel a lack of dignity if, for example, they can no longer climb the stairs, of if they have a house-training accident indoors.

The decision to have a dog put to sleep should be based on the dog's ability to cope with the processes of ageing, rather than your *inability* to cope! Just because he may be a bit smelly, or not so much fun to play with, or may soil the carpet occasionally, this is not a good enough reason to end his life. Sadly, that is the premise on which some people decide to have their dog put to sleep – perhaps we should be grateful that they are not in charge of the NHS!

With my own beautiful 'Miggi', a Bernese Mountain Dog of ten and a half years, the decision was made with complete clarity when it was apparent that, after slowly declining for the previous year, her body had finally given up on her. She had a chronic liver condition which was being managed well with medication, and her arthritic joints were being kept mobile, again with medication. Came the day when she did not want to get up for breakfast, could not even give me a wag of her tail, and I knew immediately that she had had enough. It may well be that we could have asked the vet to give her treatment that may have prolonged her life for a week or two, and which may have helped my husband and me by putting off the inevitable, but it certainly would not have done Miggi any favours. Fortunately, we have a superb vet who came to the house so quickly, and Miggi left this life with dignity, in her own home with her 'humans' by her side.

If you have heard any horror stories of how a dog is put to sleep, please cast them from your mind. The vet will usually inject the dog with an overdose of barbiturate, which is a type of anaesthetic, and the dog literally "goes to sleep". It is done with dignity, sympathy and understanding, and the last act that you can do for your dog is to make sure that you are there, holding him, when his life finally ends.

12

SOME OF THE MORE POPULAR BREEDS

The top three breeds in the UK are, in order, the Labrador, the German Shepherd (Alsatian) and the West Highland White Terrier (Westie). As a Dog Trainer, I see many examples of these and the other more popular breeds, and as such I would probably try to talk most people out of owning any of them, simply because I see more of the ones who have problems! I see the results of either illogical treatment by the owners, or of the wrong choice made, or the outcome of people breeding dogs for money, and breeding from unsuitable stock, rather than to improve their particular breed.

Obviously, there are some lovely examples of all the different breed types – and crossbreeds. To help you perhaps finally make up your mind which dog to pick, I have asked some owners to relate their own experience of living with and owning some of the more popular breeds. I asked them to be honest, and give the negative side as well as the positive side to having their particular breed within their family. I have added my own comments after each "testimonial".

Bichon Frise
"I have two of these dogs – a two year old bitch called "Phoebe" and a nine month old puppy called "Fabs". I find them delightful little dogs; intelligent, full of fun and good with children. Fabs is inclined to panic at unknown sights and

Bichon Frise.

sounds but Phoebe is much more placid and will investigate and bark at anything. They are good guard dogs, as they have a big bark for such a small dog – (they say "WOOF WOOF", not "YAP YAP") – and they have excellent hearing.

"Grooming is probably one of the biggest disadvantages and expenses of owning this breed. They need to be combed every day, which takes about fifteen minutes. They don't moult, but need to be clipped every six weeks at the grooming parlour. They also need to be bathed regularly, as they are all-white dogs and can get very dirty. My two have been taught properly to stand and be groomed and to be bathed, and so thoroughly enjoy the experience, but if you had a dog who did not enjoy it, I imagine it would make life very difficult!

"They are both rather faddy eaters, and eat slowly. They are not keen on proprietary brand dog foods, so I tend to give them fresh, home cooked meat or chicken, with potatoes, vegetables and gravy. They are fed twice a day, morning and evening.

"Training them to be obedient was relatively easy, as they enjoyed the titbits and fuss when they "got it right", although, like many dogs, they choose not to understand sometimes! House-training was not so easy, and the younger one still has the odd accident indoors. They enjoy the company of other dogs, irrespective of their size, and mix well with people.

They also get on well with the family cat.

"They like going out for walks, but Fabs hates wind and rain and just won't walk in bad weather. Neither of them likes the car very much, but since getting a travelling cage, they are now no longer sick and can travel a couple of hundred miles.

"To sum up, I would say they are very loving dogs, and are devoted to the members of their family. They love to be cuddled, to sit on laps and to sleep on the bed, and overall are utterly charming companions."

This owner has given a very honest account of living with her Bichons. She has worked hard on training, and has adopted a sensible attitude to having small dogs, not treating them like babies or toys. Because of the white fur, they are a fairly high maintenance dog, so you must find the time to bathe and groom them regularly, or have the money to pay a grooming parlour to do the job for you. The behavioural problems with small dogs are usually initiated by the owners, who sometimes forget that, whatever the size, he is still a DOG.

Border Collies
"The Border Collie is the workaholic of the dog world. Bred for generations to herd sheep in areas where it would be

Border Collie.

impossible to farm without a dog, where stamina and intelligence need to be matched with strength of character, this breed is now exported all over the world and is well known for its working ability. The versatility of the collie is also demonstrated in the way he can turn his paw to a variety of other jobs such as Search and Rescue, as well as excelling in Obedience, Agility and Working Trials.

"To the layman it would then seem logical that such a talented breed would therefore make an ideal pet. However, the very virtues that help to make them the ideal working dog can result in just the opposite. Border Collies have insatiable curiosity and energy and need considerable exercise. Not just physical exercise either – many a misguided owner has tried to calm their dog down by giving them plenty of free running, only to have ended up with a super-fit hooligan instead! Living with a Collie is a little like having a hyper-active, gifted child – they need attention, problems to solve and a leader they can respect.

"It is true that Border Collies are intelligent and learn quickly. Over the generations they have been selected for this ability, as few shepherds have the time or resources to coach the slow starters. Much of the training that they do receive serves to bring out natural instincts that are well fixed in the breed. In a pet home these instincts can be aroused by quick movement, shadows, other animals, children and even cars. These can be seen in circling, fixations, chasing, nipping and other unwanted activities. Border Collies can learn undesirable behaviour as readily as they learn the things that we intend to teach them – they are masters at reading body language and have incredibly quick reactions.

"Many Border Collies end up being re-homed or put down through no fault of their own, because their owners, often well-meaning, have failed to appreciate what they are taking on. If you want to live with a Border Collie, do your research carefully. Avoid buying at the farm gate, and find a litter that has been bred from a bitch with a sensible temperament. Start training early, find a good training class and be prepared to spend a considerable amount of time playing with and training your dog. Find out as much as you can about the breed so that you understand the instincts that drive your dog, and use them to your advantage. Remember that Collies often live to 15 years old or more, so the foundations that you build in puppyhood will be with you for many years to come''.

This owner has lived with and trained Border Collies for over thirty years, and her description of them is absolutely spot on. Unless you are committed to working your Border Collie, either in the obedience ring, working trials or agility, they are not suitable as just a 'pet' dog.

Boxers

Boxer.

''He arrived in my home aged 8 weeks old, took one look at my big, gentle Irish Wolfhound of 5 years old, and barked at him. We of course laughed, but little did we realise then that the pattern was set – ''Arnie'' decided that his purpose in life was to entertain his human family at every opportunity, and to sort out any dog he didn't like the look of!

''As he grew, so did his boldness. In my opinion, the difference between an aggressive dog and a fighter is the size of their "victim". Arnie falls into the latter group – small dogs have nothing to fear from him and with puppies he is the perfect 'uncle'. However, bigger dogs are a different ball game. He has never bitten any dog (or human), but is the canine equivalent of a stroppy teenager out on a Saturday night looking for bother. Always bigger than him, the dogs which Arnie doesn't like are easy to spot, usually breeds which themselves have a reputation – Rottweilers, Dobermans, German Shepherd Dogs, Japanese Akitas – I have never been sure if he isn't just reliving World War Two single-pawed!

"Having learnt to live with this one albeit serious character blip, the pluses and pleasures connected with living with Arnie are immeasurable. He gives love, loyalty and devotion which is second to none. He is totally protective and committed. Anyone who visits the house for the first time is subjected to his scrutiny, when he will sit firmly at my feet, between me and the caller. However, my friends soon become his, especially little girls, and he has learnt the art of looking cute, resulting in people almost falling over themselves to give him a titbit. Even now, at 12 years old, he still has the "Arrgh" factor.

"If other dogs are not on Arnie's list of loves (apart from his special canine friends) cats can do no wrong in his eyes – and not just his own house cat, who he happily allows to share his bed. Any of the neighbourhood cats are welcomed into our house and garden by Arnie, where they can stay as long as they like.

"Most Boxers have strong personalities and Arnie is no exception – he has a very strong character and can sometimes be wilful. At training classes he quickly became the class clown. Coming back to me, to be rewarded by a titbit and a cuddle, was nowhere near as rewarding as visiting all the other owners first; perhaps popping his head around the kitchen door to say hello to anyone making tea was much more fun.

"Arnie has had to learn to adapt to many changes within the household. As a younger dog, he had the company of my children. Now, with them all having flown the nest, it is just me and him, but he seems perfectly happy, welcoming them home when they visit, but resigned and accepting that they will leave again. The plus side is that Arnie and I have enjoyed many holidays together, staying in dog friendly guest houses and hotels all over England. All in all, he seems very content to be with me, and I am just so grateful to have the opportunity of sharing my life, my settee and occasionally (when he gets fed up with his own) the end of my bed, with a Boxer.''

As this lady's experiences prove, Boxers are real characters and vie for the title of clown of the dog world. I have encountered some truly lovely boxers, but also a fair proportion of those I have met have been dog aggressive, so choose the temperament very carefully if this is the breed for you. Not for the faint hearted, nor for the easily embarrassed, and certainly not for the shrinking violets!

Cocker Spaniels – Two Different Owners' Viewpoints

Cocker Spaniel.

Toffee

"I wanted a dog who would get on with my grandchildren, who are always visiting the house. I liked the look of the Cocker Spaniel but was worried about their reputation for being a bit snappy. I eventually found a breeder who was breeding from carefully chosen stock, with the specific aim of improving temperament, and as a result I chose Toffee, named after the colour of his coat.

"As a puppy, Toffee wasn't that lively; in fact the only game he really enjoyed was "chase" – first stealing a sock or a duster, and then getting the children to chase him around the house. He was not an easy puppy to train, toilet training in particular was an arduous business! Even now, at 8 years old, when I am displeased with him he simply wags his tail. Toffee's guiding force is food – he once stole the Christmas Turkey – and on walks he will scavenge anything dead. He is quite lazy, and during the daytime is happiest sleeping on the sofa in the sunshine. He tolerates other dogs, but prefers their owners, knowing that his gentle eyes and sweet face will usually win him a biscuit! He is a bit of an enigma, but we love him very much."

Daisy

"The first few years living with Daisy posed the problem of how to meet her high energy demands without overexciting her – not easy when you have children around. Even now, at 7 years old, visiting new places with Daisy can be very demanding. She has always been very vocal, barking at unfamiliar sounds or when wanting attention.

"She appears content to be left alone in her own home, but she panics if left in anyone else's house and will try to dig her way out. Her hunting instinct is very strong and I need to be one step ahead of her or she is liable to take off after the smell of deer, pheasant or cat!

"Grooming can be hard unless she is regularly clipped, otherwise her coat matts, collecting thorns and grass seeds etc. Temperamentally, she adores people, and is fairly submissive with other dogs."

In recent years, Cocker Spaniels have had a bit of a reputation for being aggressive. I think that breeders are addressing the problem now, and those which have attended my training club over the past couple of years have certainly not been too problematical. I would be doubtful about introducing them to very young children, however, and perhaps Cockers are not the best choice for first-time owners.

Crossbreeds

"I have found that one of the main differences between owning pedigree dogs and crossbred dogs is to my bank balance! All my dogs have been individual and special, no matter what their parentage or lineage, but, on the whole, I have found that the crossbreeds have been much hardier and more intelligent, although I have to say that I have found no difference in the loyalty and love given.

" 'Willie', the current oldest of my dogs, is a Staffordshire Bull Terrier-Whippet cross, and both breeds are very evident in his character and appearance. He is loyal, fast, strong and can be very protective at times. Due to ill treatment in his previous home, he is unable to be left alone and is very sensitive. He can shown signs of nervousness – possibly from the Whippet side of his parentage, and can occasionally be belligerent. In spite of being badly treated before he came to me, he loves people totally once he really gets to know them, and is beside himself with joy when my son is around.

" 'Woody', also a rescued dog, is a Labrador-Greyhound cross. He has a deep barrelled chest, and has the appearance of a Labrador, but more finely built. He is extremely sociable, lovable and unaware of his size when galloping up to greet people. He was born with a bone condition called Metaphysical Osteopathy (the result of crossing a chunky Labrador with the long legged, deep chested Greyhound), which affects his back legs. This causes him to be very prone to arthritis and as a result he does not have a great deal of stamina, making him the exception to the rule when it comes to crossbreeds being stronger and healthier than pedigrees. He has the sweetest nature and loves everyone, especially children.

" 'Elbie', yet another rescued dog, is a Chihuahua-Yorkshire Terrier cross. She looks more like a Yorkshire Terrier, but has the big eyes and feathered ears of the Chihuahua. She is fearless, friendly and is the best house dog of the three. She adores children and has never growled or curled her lip at anyone. She plays hard with the two bigger dogs and puts them in their place when necessary. She has all the ratting traits of the Yorkie and will 'kill' socks and towels by shaking them hard, as she would a rat to break its neck. She will take as much or as little exercise as is offered, and is at her happiest when sitting on someone's lap.''

It is obviously impossible to generalise about crossbreeds, simply because the variety is so huge and probably inexhaustible. This lady has three totally different types of dog, yet all are classed as crossbreeds. I have also owned crossbreeds – two Collie-Labrador crosses – and, although litter brothers, they were very different in temperament, as one took on more of the Collie character, whilst the other was typically Labrador. The definite plus was that they lived to a good age – 13 years and 16 years respectively.

Dalmatians
''We live with two Dalmatians. ''Rusper'' is 9 years old and has been with us since he was 8 weeks old. He is very docile and likes a quiet life. He is obedient when out unless he spies anything that may be edible, at which point he becomes

Dalmatian.

completely impervious to all commands! He was well socialised as a puppy and is happy to meet any other dogs. On the
whole he is very placid but extremely lovable and is adored by
all the family.

"Penny is something else! A very typical Dalmatian, active
and alert at all times. We acquired her from Dalmatian Rescue
when she was 2 years old, and we have had her for 4 years. It
was apparent that she had not been well trained, and considered herself top dog in every respect. She fought with Rusper
at first, and both my husband and I were bitten when we tried
to stop the fights. I took her to training classes, which have
helped her to become more sociable, but we still have to take
care when meeting dogs she doesn't know – in particular she
seems to hate Jack Russell Terriers. She is very good with
adults, but I would not trust her with children and she has tried
to bite our grandchildren when they are noisy or rushing
about, so we supervise any interaction very carefully.

"One of the problems in the breed is deafness, which is
genetic. Make sure that the breeder you are considering
buying from is breeding from dogs which have been tested, to
ensure that they do not produce deaf puppies. Fortunately,
neither of our dogs has a hearing problem (except when it suits
them!).

"Dalmatians are extremely adept at stealing food – nothing
is safe that is even remotely edible. Our two have stolen
chocolate in vast quantities (which is extremely bad for dogs),
a kilo bag of cat biscuits, bait from fishermen and even
complete fish. Fortunately, they have managed to devour all of
this, and more, without so far having any ill effects. Whenever
Dalmatian owners meet, we swap stories of whose dog has
managed the most spectacular theft!

"I would not recommend that a first time dog owner takes
on a Dalmatian, even though I love the breed and would never
have any other. They are certainly not the easiest of dogs to
train, they need plenty of exercise (at least two good walks a
day, and in *all* weathers) and, if not exercised enough, will
become overweight, even more restless indoors and probably
destructive too.''

This is a 'feet on the ground' opinion of living with these dogs. They have become very popular once again, due to certain recent films, and if you are considering getting one, please look beyond their pretty appearance. I see quite a few Dalmatians at my classes, and it is rare to find a dog who is aggressive towards people, although some of the males can be a bit pushy with other dogs.

German Shepherd Dogs (GSDs or Alsatians) – Two Different Owners' Viewpoints

German Shepherd.

"Foley"

"You will need a great deal of time, patience and energy to reap the positive benefits of owning a GSD. If you get it right, the loyalty and affection they give to their owner is second to none.

"I would not recommend them if you have children, even though I have a child. I have had to teach my son to respect my dog and to understand that Foley needs his own space sometimes, within the family. Of course, I have also had to train Foley to respect my son, but I have never left them alone unsupervised, and, although Foley adores children, I have to be very observant when my son has his friends round, as children can quite innocently provoke dogs.

"German Shepherds need a great deal of mental stimulation as well as physical exercise, although running free should be limited until the dog is around a year old. My own dog is long coated, and needs brushing daily to prevent the coat from getting matted, but even the short-coated types need grooming at least a couple of times a week.

"Some of my visitors are frightened of Foley, even though he is very well trained, and that is something to be taken into account when thinking of buying a GSD."

"Sadie", "Megan", "Brodie", "Skye" and "Annie"

"Having owned German Shepherds for twenty-two years, I believe that the breed is unsurpassed for showing loyalty and dedication. However, you have to be the right temperament yourself to live with such a spirited and alert breed. They thrive on physical and mental stimulation, love human inter-action and need to feel part of the family; of course, knowing their place within that family is vital.

"If you really want a GSD, seek advice from other owners, try and spend some time with their dogs and ask lots of questions so that you can get a 'feel' for what it is really like to own one of these beautiful dogs. Go and see several breeders before you finally make your choice. Make sure that both the dam and sire of the puppy you choose are free from any possible hereditary conditions such as epilepsy and hip dysplasia.

"I owned my first dog before my children were born, and introducing them requires a great deal of care and common sense. The dog needs to know where he stands within the family and it is important that he does not feel rejected when a baby comes along. As my sons grew, the bond between them and the first and subsequent new canine additions developed, as did mutual respect. My boys were never allowed to tease or torment the dogs – young children cannot understand that dogs have feelings and can have an "off" day. I never allowed boisterous or noisy interaction between the children and the dogs – it is far too easy for accidents to occur.

"I have found GSDs to be very biddable with training, provided that you are logical and kind – harsh training will simply provoke the dog into acting defensively. Exercise was limited until my dogs were about a year old, and they were not allowed to run up or down stairs, as this can damage young growing bones. The GSD wants to learn – getting involved in obedience and agility provides them with physical and mental exercise, plus it is a great way to meet other like-minded owners.

"The breed does have a reputation for being "standoffish" with strangers and other dogs. I have not experienced this myself, as I have always socialised my puppies thoroughly, taking them with me to meet my children from school, and actively involving them in our family life. All my dogs, past and present, have given my family enormous pleasure, and for me they are *the* most impressive breed."

Both of these owners have painted a very accurate picture of GSDs. Often, these dogs are obtained for the wrong reasons, maybe as a guard dog or simply because they are impressive to look at and as such some people like the reaction they provoke. GSDs can be quite vocal, and often appear nervous of people or situations of which they are unsure. Unless you're really sure about what you're taking on, perhaps this is not the ideal dog for first time ownership.

Golden Retrievers – Three Different Owners' Viewpoints

"Jenna"
"I chose a bitch, as I had heard that the dogs could be fairly stubborn. Jenna was slow to mature, and stayed young and fun loving for a long time. She is a bit scatty at times, but was easily trained and is trustworthy with children and gentle with all people and dogs. I have met other Retrievers who were not so gentle or good tempered, and realise that picking the right breeder, plus going to training classes, is essential with this working breed.

Golden Retriever.

"She loves getting wet and her coat, being long and feathery, requires a fair bit of attention afterwards, with brushing and drying."

"George"

"George is our much loved 15 year old Golden Retriever. He has been a pleasure to live with ever since he moved in with us. As a puppy he did all the usual chewing etc, but if you leave things lying around, you have to expect that sort of thing.

"He has always had a wonderful and gentle temperament. He was easy to train, simply wanting to please, and loves children, adults and other dogs. If members of 'his' family are in different rooms in the house, he will wander back and forth between us, puffing and blowing, and is only really relaxed when we are all together again. George loves his walks, although now he is elderly can only manage a short distance. He travels very well in the car and behaves well even on long distances. Any family would feel especially blessed to have had a Golden Retriever like our George."

Since this was written, George became very frail and was subsequently put to sleep, to save him any suffering. I knew

George, and agree with everything his owners have said about him – he was an absolute poppet and a pleasure to know.

"Monty" and "Rommel"

"Once we had decided that our family should have a dog, we looked at the size and character of several breeds before deciding on a Golden Retriever. We wanted a dog that would be large enough to enjoy energetic walks, but would still fit into the confines of an urban semi. Temperamentally, the dog would have to be good with children, with an affectionate and trustworthy nature. We also wanted a dog who would not bring forth negative responses from neighbours or people in public areas. Finally, we wanted, where possible, to get a breed that did not have serious health or genetic defects. Golden Retrievers are known to have a predisposition towards hip problems, but overall we decided that this was the right breed for us.

"Once we had found a suitable breeder, we were invited to attend for an interview! The lady was extremely charming, but made it very clear that we had to prove that we would be suitable owners for one of her puppies. This required two extensive visits, before finally Monty was chosen and eventually came to live with us.

"He was an enthusiastic chewer, eating carpets, curtains and chair legs. A puppy cage (indoor kennel) proved an essential accessory, although at first we were very reluctant to use one, but the breeder strongly advised it and we were extremely grateful for such sound advice. Monty loved his den, and chewing and house-training were then much easier to control, with Monty becoming clean indoors within 2 to 3 months.

"One of the biggest problems we have encountered, both with Monty and now with our new goldie puppy Rommel, is their enthusiasm for gardening! There is nothing they enjoy more than digging up the lawn (there is now none left), uprooting all the shrubs and flowers from the flower beds, hanging by their mouths from branches of small bushes and trees, and generally creating total garden chaos! I have to admit that, as we are not committed gardeners, the sight of them playing and having such obvious fun is more than adequate compensation for the total (but hopefully temporary) destruction of our garden.

"As an indication of how two dogs of the same breed can differ, when it comes to food, Monty is a slow eater and tends to become bored with the same food after a while. Rommel, on the other hand, never shows any reluctance and will eat what we put in front of him.

"Indoors, our dogs like to lie across the middle of the hall, causing quite a sizable obstruction. They have high energy levels, jumping and running about, and when their humans are sitting down they can expect to be sat on, nuzzled, hit in the face with a feathery, wagging tail, or trodden on. Being long-haired dogs, they seem constantly to shed vast quantities of hair, and, even with regular grooming of dogs and regular vacuuming of carpets, there is still dog hair to be found. They also 'slobber', which causes unsightly stains on clothing!

"Outside, both dogs are extremely sociable, and a joy to take for a walk – the true pleasure of dog ownership for our family. We can take them anywhere, and have made many new friends as a result. The perceived image we had of Golden Retrievers was that of a loyal, loving, boisterous and friendly dog – we have certainly not been disappointed with either of our two, and they have certainly lived up to that reputation.

"We have been very fortunate both in our choice of breeder and our choice of dogs, and realise that there are bad examples of our breed too, but our experience has been such a good one that we would recommend Golden Retrievers for a family, particularly if they like walking, but do not enjoy gardening!"

Three lovely accounts of this very popular breed. All of these owners have made a point of training their dogs, so that the lovely nature of the breed has taken precedence. Untrained, they can be a bit pushy sometimes, but I have rarely come across a "people aggressive" goldie – some of the males I have encountered have been a bit stroppy with other male dogs, but this is usually because of incorrect training, especially during puppyhood.

Great Danes

Great Dane.

"Great Danes are lovable great hunks that will do their best to eat you out of house and home. They do not need as much exercise as some people think, as they have short bursts of energy and generally are content to plod around after you. In my experience their veterinary bills are proportionate to their size! They also have a short life span – anything over 7 years is a bonus, which may not be ideal for a family dog, with the ensuing heartbreak that losing them relatively early brings. They are generally very loving and gentle, but obviously, because of their size, the home has to adapted accordingly – no low tables with ornaments for a start! You also need to consider how your children's friends will feel being confronted with a dog who may be bigger than them."

Again, another very honest account of this particular breed. Perhaps for a family the high maintenance and short life span of a Great Dane is not ideal, plus being so large, interaction between the dog and the children will not be easy. I have encountered several Great Danes, and they have all been very gentle, in spite of their size.

Irish Setters (also known as Red Setters)

Irish Setter.

"I have owned Irish Setters for 25 years, and for me they are the ideal family dog. In all my years of living with this breed, I have only come across one dog with a suspect temperament, and this was with other dogs, not people.

"Many people think that Irish Setters are stupid, and that you can never get them back once you let them off the lead. This has not been my experience. If they appear to be scatty, this is due to lack of training. When taught correctly, with kind methods, you will have a fun loving and intelligent companion for the duration of the dog's life. The average lifespan is between 10 and 15 years, and they are slow to mature, not really being 'grown up' until about 7 years old.

"There are four types of setter. The Irish is red in colour, sometimes with a dash of white on the chest. The Red & White Setter is mainly white with splashes of red. The Gordon Setter – the largest of all setters – is black and tan. Finally, the English

Setter, which can be orange (brown) and white, blue (grey) and white, or tricoloured, which is white, red and brown.

"Within the Irish Setters, I have only ever had males, but for a first–time dog owner I would suggest a bitch – the males tend to be stronger, both physically and mentally. Of course, with a bitch you will have to cope with her coming into season. Spaying is the obvious answer, but bear in mind that sometimes a spayed bitch's coat may go a bit fluffy afterwards.

"The Irish Setter has a beautiful silky coat, which will need regular attention – at least twice weekly grooming sessions to prevent it becoming matted. As to exercise, you will find it hard to wear them out! Obviously, when they are puppies, and until they are about 9 months old, exercise should be limited, so that they don't damage their growing bones.

"Some Irish Setters can be fairly fussy eaters, so make sure that you get feeding advice and a diet sheet from the breeder. You should also check that, before both the dam and sire were bred from, they were both tested for the known defects within the breed, which can be passed on to their offspring. Ask about the following:

1. Mouths – an Irish Setter should have a scissor bite, i.e. the top set of teeth should fit cleanly and closely over the bottom set.
2. Eyes – Progressive Retinal Atrophy (PRA) was present in the breed a few years ago. It has now been virtually eradicated due to careful breeding, but make sure that the parents of the puppy are certified clear.
3. Canine Leucocyte Adhesion Deficiency (CLAD) is a comparatively recent problem which has affected some Irish Setters. It is an inherited immunodeficiency condition, causing various severe recurrent infections in the young dog, which respond poorly to antibiotics. The young dog gets progressively weaker, usually leading to euthanasia before the dog is six months old. The mutation associated with the severe form of CLAD has recently been identified and a DNA based test for carrier detection is now available.

4. Irish Setters, being fairly large dogs, are also at risk from Gastric Dilation, so the necessary precautions should be taken when feeding your dog. (See Chapter 9, page 109).

"Provided you take every precaution when choosing a breeder, your puppy should come to you in glowing health. Once you are the proud owner of this truly lovely breed, you will be addicted for life. They have beauty, intelligence and an enormous capacity for getting the very best out of life."

A very knowledgeable account from this owner, who clearly knows her breed. I have personally never met a bad tempered Setter, but they are not a breed for those who like a quiet, sedentary life!

Labradors – Two Owners' Viewpoints

Labrador.

"Kelly" and "Poppy"
"Having had two, I would best describe them as being a bit like a bull in a china shop. Finesse does not spring to mind! Kelly was my first, followed later by Poppy, both Yellow

Labradors. They were reasonably easy to train, but I have only ever had bitches, and talking to owners of male Labradors I have learned that the boys can be more difficult. They need lots of interesting exercise – a walk around a town park is not enough, and generally they are sociable with both people and other dogs, but will retaliate if another dog pushes them too far. Training needs to be kept interesting, or they quickly get bored. Coat care is easy – being short coated a good brushing a couple of times a week is sufficient.''

"Cassie" and "Stanley"

"When we decided to have Cassie and Stanley, brother and sister Black Labradors, we did not know that having two puppies together was not a very good idea! The first twelve months were quite difficult, mainly because we were never sure who had done what! Cassie is more obedient – she likes to play with a ball during our walks. Stanley is more difficult, as he can't resist going to see all of the other dogs, even if they are a long way away. Now he is older we don't panic so much, as he will now come back to us once he has said his ''hello''s.

"They are big, solid dogs, and tend to walk through things rather than around them. They have both knocked us over when playing and not looking where they were going. This boisterous behaviour can be a bit of a worry if there are young children around, although they are completely non-aggressive and love children and adults alike.

"They need loads of exercise and even after a long walk will still career around the house for a while before they crash out for a couple of hours. They love travelling in the car, and we hardly know they're there, as they are so good. The pleasure and entertainment they give us outweighs the problems, but I would certainly not recommend getting two puppies together, and will not do it again.''

As Labradors are currently the number one breed in the UK, it is understandable that I see more of them at my training club than any other breed. They are not as trainable for the pet home as the Golden Retriever, and the males especially can sometimes be difficult. They come in three colours: yellow, black and chocolate. They are extremely energetic dogs, especially as puppies, and need early training to channel their energies into things which you like them doing, rather than things you don't like!

Springer Spaniels (Welsh)

Springer Spaniel.

"Having had Welsh Springers for many years, my advice is don't get one if you're easily embarrassed or very houseproud! At training classes, you will be the owner with the reddest face as your dog will think of at least three other things he'd rather do than the thing you are asking of him. He will not look at you adoringly whilst walking to heel, as he will be too busy sniffing the floor or the dog nearest to him. On walks he will jump into all available muddy water – the smellier the better! He will go off hunting rabbits and pheasants, and will track them for miles. He will need lots of exercise – he was bred to work all day.

"At home, he will follow you and be at your side whenever possible, so must be trained carefully to accept that sometimes he must remain in one room whilst you are in another, otherwise he will develop separation anxiety. If you are working full-time you should not contemplate getting a Welsh Springer – they are such a sociable breed and thrive on human company. He will need to have his feet and ears trimmed regularly, so you will need to learn how to do this, or take him to a grooming parlour.

"A Welsh Springer will adore you, greet you with wild enthusiasm, won't go looking for trouble from other dogs, but will be courageous if provoked. If you're lucky he will live to about 12 years old, starting to slow down at about 8 years old. He will love everyone and will be a happy, outgoing character."

A lovely working breed, which is fairly adaptable to living within a family, provided they are not left to their own devices for long periods of time. This owner knows her breed and her description of their character is extremely accurate. The Welsh Springer, and their cousin the English Springer, are very energetic and amusing dogs, and will make good family pets provided they are properly trained and given sufficient exercise.

West Highland White (Westie)
"I chose a Westie because of the way they look and because of their size. Having now owned one for nearly two years, I

West Highland White.

wouldn't change "Sophie" for anything, but if I was considering having a second dog, I wouldn't have another Westie – I think one is more than enough for any family!

"Her good points . . . Sophie learnt quickly, which surprised me as I was apprehensive at first, with her being a terrier I had heard how difficult they can be. She really enjoyed the classes and loved the socialising with the other puppies. She will now sit, lie down and come when called, and will sit and wait nicely whilst I attach her lead. Staying when told is not one of her strong points, but she can do it, and in general is as obedient as I need her to be. She loves the company of other dogs, especially if they are bigger than her. She is very enthusiastic about going for a walk – I take her out for one on-the-lead walk a day, plus she has about half an hour running in the park daily. She still tries to pull on the lead, but is slowly getting better!

"Sophie is brushed every day – her coat is quite thick and she has not been clipped, so her coat can get matted if not looked after. She also has a bath at least every six weeks. Fortunately, she enjoys both these activities. Westies are particularly prone to flea allergies, so I have to ensure that flea prevention treatment is regularly applied.

"Her not so good points . . . As far as Sophie is concerned, cats are for chasing – she doesn't hurt them, but just seems to enjoy the chase. If they stop running, so does she. She is very jealous of our cats, and does not like it when one of them is on my lap – she will continually try to get my attention until eventually the cat goes away. I would not trust her with any small animals such as guinea pigs, hamsters or rabbits, as sadly she did kill our hamster.

"Sophie considers that the garden is solely there for her to excavate, and the lawn is now covered with masses of holes. She also barks at every single noise when she is outside, and also barks a fair bit indoors too – noises on the TV will start her off. However, when we visit friends or family, she does not bark in their houses or gardens.

"I have four children, the oldest being 13 years and the youngest 4 years. I do not think that Westies are particularly good with children, and would not recommend them with children under 10 years old. Sophie has snapped at my two youngest children and will grumble at them if they come near me when she is beside me. She is also very possessive with food, whether it is hers or food left on the table, and will sit beside it and growl at the cats or the children if they go near it. The only person she does not growl at in the family is me, whom she seems to idolise, following me everywhere I go.

"Whether some of these bad points are to do with her breeding, or whether it is simply that I did not understand the breed enough, I'm not sure. I would not want to be without her, but she is certainly not the easiest dog to live with."

This is a real 'warts and all' account of living with this tough little dog. They are now very popular, but you must be aware that they like to dominate and need logical and early training to get the best out of them. Coat care can be demanding, and their activity ratio is not in proportion to their size!

Yorkshire Terrier

Yorkshire Terrier.

" 'Barney' was my first pet and for a year it was just him, until two more dogs and three cats joined the family. Even as a small puppy he was fearless and is completely undaunted by larger dogs. He is good natured, patient, obedient and rarely growls. He does bark at other dogs when out for walks, rushing up to them in a bossy manner and telling them in no uncertain terms to mind their Ps and Qs, but is not aggressive and soon makes friends with canines and humans alike.

"He has plenty of energy and copes very well with long walks. He has an obsession with chasing balls, and once he has retrieved a ball will do everything in his power to hang on to it. My sons have named him "Sniper" because of his deadly accuracy when snatching a ball from their hands.

"He has a long coat which if kept unclipped requires a huge amount of grooming, so I have Barney regularly clipped, as I do not want to show him.

"All in all he is a loyal and loving pet, and holds a very special place in my heart."

This lady has treated her dog as a dog, not as a toy, and so has extracted the very best out of him. Too often, these tiny dogs are treated as ornaments, and end up pampered and spoilt. Because of their size, they could be at risk if you have clumsy children around, and they do not take well to being mauled about.

I hope that reading these personal experiences of some of the breeds has helped you. I am sure that for every positive comment made about a particular breed, someone else would make a negative one, and vice versa. Choosing the right breeder, and then raising the puppy in a logical (for the dog) way is vital.

There is a huge variety of dogs to choose from, and the following lists include most of the better known breeds, under their various groups. Obviously to write about each of them individually would take at least another half dozen books, so when you choose the breed you like the sound of, start doing your homework and find out everything you can.

Whether you choose a pedigree or crossbreed, I hope you find this book has helped with that initial decision, and will continue to help throughout your dog owning life.

SPORTING BREEDS

HOUNDS
– Dogs bred for hunting by trailing or by sight.

Basenji
Basset Hound
Beagle
Bloodhound

Bloodhound.

Borzoi
Dachshund – Long-haired, Miniature Long-haired, Smooth-
  haired, Wire-haired, Miniature Wire-haired
Deerhound
Elkhound
Finnish Spitz
Foxhound
Greyhound
Hamiltonstovare
Ibizan Hound
Irish Wolfhound
Otterhound
Pharaoh Hound
Rhodesian Ridgeback
Saluki
Whippet

GUNDOGS
**– Bred for either hunting, pointing, flushing out game or
retrieving. Some of the breeds are multi-purpose, incor-
porating some or all of these traits.**

Brittany Spaniel
English Setter
German Short-haired Pointer
German Wire-haired Pointer
Gordon Setter
Hungarian Vizla
Hungarian Wire-haired Vizla
Irish Red and White Setter
Irish Setter
Italian Spinone
Large Munsterlander
Pointer
Retriever – Chesapeake Bay, Curly Coated, Flat Coated,
  Golden, Labrador

English Setter.

Spaniel – American Cocker, Cavalier King Charles, King
    Charles Spaniel, Clumber Spaniel, English Springer, Welsh
    Springer, English Cocker, Field, Irish Water, Sussex
Weimaraner

TERRIERS
**– Dogs bred to assist mankind in various forms of vermin
control, some for digging out quarry, some for following
horses and then going to ground, digging out foxes,
badgers, martens, rats, etc.**

Airedale Terrier
Australian Terrier
Bedlington Terrier
Bull Terrier – Miniature, English, Staffordshire
Cairn Terrier
Dandie Dinmont Terrier
English Toy Terrier
Fox Terrier – Smooth, Wire-coated
Glen of Imaal Terrier

Irish Terrier
Jack Russell Terrier

Jack Russell.

Kerry Blue Terrier
Lakeland Terrier
Maltese Terrier
Manchester Terrier
Norfolk Terrier
Norwich Terrier
Parson Jack Russell Terrier
Scottish Terrier
Sealyham Terrier
Skye Terrier
Soft-Coated Wheaten Terrier
Welsh Terrier
West Highland White Terrier
Yorkshire Terrier

NON–SPORTING BREEDS

WORKING DOGS
– Bred to guard and protect either livestock, property or people, and sometimes to attack where necessary. Some also used as drove dogs.

Alaskan Malamute
Bernese Mountain Dog
Bouvier des Flandres
Boxer
Bullmastiff
Doberman
Eskimo Dog
Giant Schnauzer
Great Dane
Hovawart
Leonburger
Mastiff
Neopolitan Mastiff
Newfoundland
Pinscher
Portuguese Water Dog
Rottweiler
St. Bernard
Siberian Husky
Tibetan Mastiff

Doberman.

PASTORAL
– Dogs bred for herding and/or driving cattle and sheep.

Anatolian Shepherd Dog
Australian Cattle Dog
Bearded Collie
Belgian Shepherd Dog
Border Collie
Briard
Collie – Rough, Smooth
Estrela Mountain Dog
German Shepherd Dog (Alsatian)
Hungarian Kuvasz
Hungarian Puli
Komondor
Lancashire Heeler
Maremma Sheepdog
Norwegian Buhund
Old English Sheepdog
Polish Lowland Sheepdog
Pyrenean Mountain Dog

Old English Sheepdog.

Samoyed
Shetland Sheepdog
Swedish Vallhund
Welsh Corgi – Cardigan, Pembroke

UTILITY
– Dogs bred for a variety of different purposes, ranging from fighting bulls, hunting bear and deer, pulling sledges and carts, gundogs, and some simply for ornament.

Boston Terrier
Bulldog
Chow Chow
Dalmatian
French Bulldog
German Spitz
Japanese Akita
Japanese Shiba Inu
Japanese Spitz
Keeshond
Lhasa Apso

Bulldog.

Miniature Schnauzer
Poodle – Standard, Miniature & Toy
Schipperke
Schnauzer
Shar Pei
Shih Tzu
Tibetan Spaniel
Tibetan Terrier

TOY DOGS
– Some toy dogs have been included in the specific categories already listed, such as the Yorkshire Terrier, which is included in the Terrier list. The following toy dogs do not fit within the guidelines of the other groups, not having been bred or used for a specific task. Some of them have origins within other larger breeds and have been deliberately bred smaller and smaller, until the size required was arrived at, making them more suitable for being a pet or lap dog.

Chihuahua – Long coat, Smooth coat
Chinese Crested
Griffon Bruxellois
Italian Greyhound

Chihuahua.

Japanese Chin
Miniature Pinscher
Papillon
Pekingese
Pomeranian
Pug

APPENDIX –
USEFUL ADDRESSES

Barjo Engineering – suppliers of indoor kennels, extension
panels and car cages
Birchin Inhams Farm, Heathlands Road, Wokingham, Berk-
shire, RG40 3AP.
Tel: 0118 9890240
Web: www.burfey.net/barjo

Breed Rescues
Most veterinary surgeries have lists of individual breed rescues, or these can be obtained from the Kennel Club.

Dog Training Weekly – weekly canine magazine
Print House, Parc Y Shwt, Fishguard, Dyfed, SA65 9AP.

Dog World – weekly canine magazine
Somerfield House, Wotton Road, Ashford, Kent, TN23 6LW.

The Kennel Club
The Kennel Club, 1 Clarges Street, London, W1Y 8AB.
Tel: 0870 606 6750
E-Mail: info@the-kennel-club.org.uk
Web: www.the-kennel-club.org.uk

The National Canine Defence League (NCDL)
NCDL Head Office, 17 Wakley Street, London, EC1V 7RQ.
Tel: 020 7837 0006
Fax: 020 7833 2701
Web: www.ncdl.org.uk

Our Dogs – weekly canine magazine
5 Oxford Road, Station Approach, Manchester, M60 1SX.

Pet Travel Scheme (PETS)
Web: www.maff.gov.uk/animalh/quarantine/index.htm

**The Royal Society for the Prevention of Cruelty to
  Animals (RSPCA)**
Enquiries Service, RSPCA, Causeway, Horsham, West Sussex,
RH12 1HG.
General enquiries: 0870 444 3127
Emergency 24 hour hotline: 0870 5555 999
E-Mail: info@rspca.org.uk
Web: www.rspca.org.uk

INDEX